UNLOCKING EXECUTIVE FUNCTIONING SKILLS FOR TEENS

Simple Tools To Improve Focus,
Beat Procrastination, And Thrive In High School

KIMBERLY MYRICK

DEDICATION PAGE

For every teen who's ever felt overwhelmed,
scattered, or stuck, you're capable of more than you know,
and you've got this.

ACKNOWLEDGEMENT

Writing this book has been a journey, and I couldn't have done it alone.

Thank you to the ones who gave their unwavering support, patience, and encouragement. Your belief in me, even on the toughest days, made all the difference.

To my editor, designer, and everyone involved in bringing this book to life, your expertise and dedication helped shape these pages into something truly meaningful. I'm grateful for your hard work and attention to detail.

CONTENT

INTRODUCTION

H ave you ever woken up on a school day convinced that this time today you'll be on top of everything? You're sure you'll conquer your homework, respond to all your messages, handle that group project, and maybe even have time to just chill. But then life happens: you forget an important assignment until lunchtime, your phone pulls you into scrolling for hours, and by the evening, you're too exhausted to do any of it. Sound familiar?

If you've been there more than once, you're not alone. We've all been there thinking we can handle everything but ending up feeling behind, stressed, and overwhelmed. You are certainly among many who experienced this situation repeatedly. Your daily responsibilities create a difficult juggling situation because schoolwork, sports activities, household tasks, your part-time position and maintaining friendships compete for your time. Life's responsibilities become overwhelming because trying hard does not prevent feeling behind. Executive functioning capabilities help people achieve their goals.

During your teen years, these abilities are more important than ever. High school brings new responsibilities, and as you prepare for college and juggle social activities, sports, clubs, and maybe even a job, executive functioning can make all the difference in keeping things from becoming overwhelming.

THE BENEFITS YOU'LL GET FROM THIS BOOK

The book provides readers with hands-on methods to enhance their executive functioning skills. Your brain consists of executive functions, which act as the mental system that allows planning, organization, and time management along with emotional regulation, resulting in the smooth performance of brain functions. People without these skills encounter major difficulties when performing basic activities such as homework submission and practice attendance. Learning such abilities helps you to handle your life situations better until you reach a state of being in control.

In this book, you will learn how to overcome procrastination alongside essential skills such as time management and goal setting, as well as emotional control and effective communication. You'll find real life examples, simple exercises, and reflection questions sprinkled throughout. This isn't just a book you read and forget; it's more like a personal coach that nudges you to try things, notice what works, and fine-tune your approach.

WHO THIS BOOK IS FOR?

This book is designed for teens who want straightforward, practical advice they can use immediately. Whether you're dealing with school, sports, family responsibilities, a part-time job, or simply trying to live with more calm and efficiency, the tools in this book will help. Parents, counsellors, and educators may also find it helpful to understand how to support teens in developing executive functioning skills. Ultimately, this book is for you to give you the tools to feel more confident, in control, and capable of handling whatever life throws your way.

OUR APPROACH

We'll begin by exploring the basics of executive functioning and how brain development plays a big role in it. Then, we'll tackle time management, organization, focus, emotional regulation, goal setting, and communication. Along the way, you'll encounter short stories of other teens dealing with challenges like procrastination and scheduling overload, as well as invitations to try out exercises and reflect on your own experiences. Remember, this isn't just about reading, it's about doing. And by the time you finish, you'll have a toolkit of strategies that will help you navigate everything from final exams to job applications, big family blowouts, to late-night essay crises.

No matter where you're starting from, know this: executive functioning isn't about being naturally organized or good at multitasking. It's a skill set you can develop, just like building muscle. So take heart you don't have to stick with the habits that aren't working for you. With practice and the right strategies, you can gain control of your life and feel more confident in the process. Ready to begin? Let's get started and learn more about executive functioning, starting with what's going on in your teen brain and why it's more important than you might imagine.

CHAPTER 1

UNDERSTANDING EXECUTIVE FUNCTIONING

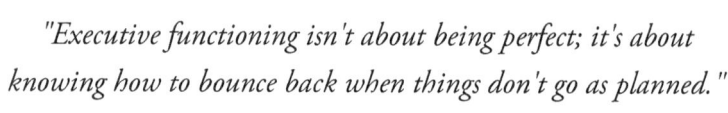

"Executive functioning isn't about being perfect; it's about knowing how to bounce back when things don't go as planned."
— Kimberly Myrick

Consider being the CEO of your own organization. As the CEO, you will need to supervise different departments while controlling deadlines to ensure operational success. Your brain serves as the organization that needs attention. You maintain control of your academic responsibilities together with your club activities, social commitments, and domestic duties throughout the day. Smooth operations within the system lead to tasks disappearing and deadlines approaching suddenly while producing intense stress.

The mental system known as executive functioning enables you to organize and plan while focusing on important tasks until you accomplish them. Strong executive functioning skills make you feel like you successfully manage your daily activities. Weak executive functioning skills create a feeling where you remain perpetually behind schedule while rushing to maintain your position.

The ability to build executive functioning skills does not depend on your birthright. You can develop this skill set through practice in the same way you learn new sports or musical instruments.

This chapter explains executive functioning basics while showing its significance and introducing approaches to enhance it right now.

THE BRAIN OPERATES AS A CEO THROUGH EXECUTIVE FUNCTIONING CONTROL SYSTEMS

Your brain operates through its control centre, known as executive functioning, which helps you decide things, establish goals and maintain your focus while managing distractions. Several essential mental abilities make up this system and include:

- **Working Memory:** It enables people to maintain and utilize information at the present moment. During math problem solving students must keep the teacher's instructions in their mind.

- **Cognitive Flexibility:** This is the ability to switch gears mentally. Ever had a teacher change the due date of a project last-minute or a coach rearrange practice times? Cognitive flexibility helps you roll with those changes without flipping out.

- **Task Initiation:** It refers to beginning tasks without motivation, even though you lack the desire to start. (Goodbye, procrastination!)

- **Impulse Control:** You need impulse control to avoid reacting to distractions that might include texting during homework or blurting out in school.

- **Emotional Regulation:** The ability to control stress together with frustration and anxiety which prevents them from dominating your actions.

All these skills function as a system where weak points disrupt the entire structure. You would face major challenges while doing homework because you experience test anxiety for emotional regulation or because your thoughts constantly shift to dinner time for impulse control. The lack of mental process coordination makes it simple to experience both stuckness and overwhelming feelings.

WHY EXECUTIVE FUNCTIONING FEELS HARD (BUT CAN BE IMPROVED)

Many students experience overwhelming deadlines while dealing with disorganization which demonstrates a widespread issue. The brain of a teenager operates with an executive functioning system that is in the process of development. The prefrontal cortex, which manages decision-making and planning functions, remains unfinished during your teenage years. Your brain operates with different levels of effectiveness between days, which explains why you may feel super productive on some days while others seem to be in a state of sleep mode.

The prefrontal cortex develops throughout your mid-20s, according to scientific findings, thus making executive functioning skills still in development. With dedicated practice, you possess the ability to enhance your executive functioning system.

The process is similar to fitness training at the gym. You must train your muscles to achieve stronger muscles. The brain functions according to this same principle. Continuous practice of executive functioning skills through organization methods, time management and goal setting will strengthen their reliability and performance.

Myths and Misconceptions

- **Myth:** Teens just don't want to do better.

- **Reality:** Motivation can fluctuate, and it's often tied to how well your executive functioning skills are developed.

- **Myth:** If you're not organized by now, you never will be.

- **Reality:** Brain plasticity means you can always improve with practice

REAL LIFE CHALLENGES AND HOW TO TACKLE THE

Caleb attends high school in his sophomore year while spending most of his time gaming instead of completing math assignments. His Call of Duty gaming sessions become so long that he ends up in a panic when he discovers he has to take a mathematics exam the following day. Inside, he understands that making a study schedule would be the right choice for him. So what's stopping him?

Caleb faces two main difficulties which include beginning his flashcard work and failing to record test dates properly in his scheduling tool. His brain functions in a manner that prioritizes receiving instant game victories above completing future assignments such as his upcoming test.

After Caleb masters basic skills to initiate tasks and schedule his tests, he feels less pressure in his life, and gaming doesn't consume all his leisure time.

His problem was solved by the following method:

★ **The Two-Minute Rule for Task Initiation**

It becomes more challenging to begin the work. Caleb states to himself that he will begin math review for just two minutes instead of waiting for motivation to appear. The process of starting any task such as writing an essay sentence or reviewing a flashcard makes subsequent continuation more achievable.

After starting your workout even when you resist it you will discover that you want to keep going because you entered your exercise flow. Any task that you wish to avoid follows the same principle.

★ **Visualize the End Result**

Struggling to focus? You will feel satisfied when you hand in your work right on time or when you finish your studies effectively. A mental adjustment triggers motivational forces.

★ **Create a Distraction-Free Zone**

Your environment affects your brain. Your ability to concentrate will deteriorate whenever your phone produces notifications while sitting next to you. Caleb decided to store his phone somewhere distant from his study area. No distractions, more focus.

★ **Break It Down**

A large project can often feel overwhelming. Caleb handles this by transforming vague thinking into specific study targets for his math exam—one day reviewing Chapter 5, the next completing five practice problems. Dividing tasks into smaller, more manageable steps keeps procrastination at bay.

★ **Self-Check Your Progress**

Caleb examines his daily achievements when he goes to bed. Maybe he needs to change his approach for the following day. Constant small changes throughout time lead to growth.

WHY MASTERING EXECUTIVE FUNCTIONING PAYS OFF

Executive functioning skills develop beyond the classroom because they influence all aspects of life. The skills enable you to tackle various life challenges by controlling both friendships and home responsibilities.

Strong executive functioning provides these four advantages to your life:

- **Academic Success:** Your academic performance will improve because you will handle assignments on schedule, learn better and minimize panic during critical deadlines.

- **More Free Time:** Effective task organization allows people to create extra free periods that let them pursue their favorite activities.

- **Better Emotional Control:** Stress management techniques will become available to you after developing better emotional control over your reactions.

- **Long-Term Benefits:** The development of solid executive functioning abilities enables people to do well in college and work as well as in their normal everyday lives.

Your Executive Functioning Self-Check

- Do I often forget deadlines?

- Do I freeze up when I have too much to do?

- Do I struggle to switch tasks or adjust when plans change?

- Do I get so stressed that I can't focus on homework?

- If you answered "yes" to any of these, you're not alone. And the best part? These challenges are fixable.

What's Next?

Moving forward, you have learned about executive functioning basics and their importance, which leads to a necessary action plan. The first step? Mastering time management.

Do you find yourself longing for additional hours in your day? Do you struggle to meet deadlines before their due dates, and do you persistently lack enough time to complete your work? You're not alone. The ability to manage time effectively stands as the strongest executive functioning skill you can learn because the following chapter will show you basic yet useful methods to control your time usage and minimize daily stress.

Chapter 2

MASTERING TIME MANAGEMENT

❖

"Time management is life management."
— *Julie Morgenstern,*

Every morning, Brent approaches his tasks with the intention of completing everything successfully. He wakes up with the belief that today will be the day he finishes homework first and practices the guitar before he watches Netflix. When night descends, he looks at his incomplete math assignment while feeling remorse for missing his guitar practice once more.

Brent possesses the capabilities yet he never acquired the skills needed to handle his time properly. And he's not alone.

Every teenager requires time management skills the way adults do because it serves as an essential life skill. Implementing time management strategies helps young adults meet their tasks effectively, which reduces their stress levels while improving their productivity. By effectively planning your time allocation you will both eliminate feelings of being overwhelmed as well as achieve better outcomes in your daily activities and preserve time for favored activities.

What steps can you take to move from always running out of time to mastering control over your schedule? Let's break it down.

WHY TIME MANAGEMENT FEELS SO HARD

Time management seems straightforward because you only need to create daily schedules which you should follow precisely. Actual life conditions such as procrastination along with distractions and inadequate planning create barriers to effective time usage. Procrastination represents the main obstacle. But why do we do it?

Why Do We Procrastinate?

When you sit down to study, you often find yourself compelled to check your phone, eat food, or scroll social media. The practice of choosing simpler, enjoyable tasks over essential ones represents procrastination.

Here's why it happens:

→ Quick rewards gain priority over future advantages because the brain functions this way. The instant pleasure of scrolling social media provides immediate satisfaction, yet studying produces benefits that will come later.

→ We avoid challenging tasks when they appear difficult to handle rather than dividing them into achievable parts.

→ The absence of motivation becomes a barrier that stops us from working even though deadlines do not apply.

The good news? Developing a better system for time management allows you to defeat procrastination.

TIME BLOCKING: STRUCTURING YOUR DAY FOR SUCCESS

Time blocking stands as the most effective method to both eliminate procrastination and gain control over your scheduling.

What Is Time Blocking?

Time blocking functions as a scheduling method which assigns particular time slots throughout the day for completing all your work obligations. You will eliminate vague to-do lists by dedicating predetermined blocks of time to each task.

How to Time Block Your Day

→ All necessary tasks need to be written down. Write down all essential activities including schoolwork and extracurriculars and personal time blocks.

→ Break your day into time slots. Each task needs its own designated period of time to accomplish. **Example:**

4:00 - 4:30 PM → Math homework

4:30 - 5:00 PM → Science reading

5:00 - 5:15 PM → Break

5:15 - 6:00 PM → Writing assignment

→ Keep the schedule but maintain flexibility when necessary. When unexpected situations occur, you should adjust your schedule rather than abandon everything.

Why It Works

- **Prevents procrastination** – When a task has a dedicated time, you're less likely to delay it.

- **Gives a clear structure** – You know exactly when you'll work and when you'll relax.

- **Reduces last-minute stress** – No more rushing assignments at the last second.

THE POMODORO TECHNIQUE & OTHER STUDY HACKS

Have you ever spent long study sessions without keeping any information in your memory? That's where the Pomodoro Technique comes in. Named after a tomato-shaped kitchen timer ("pomodoro" means tomato in Italian), this approach has you alternate between short, intense focus and quick breaks.

How the Pomodoro Technique Works

→ Choose a task which requires study for a test.

→ Start the timer for 25 minutes and stay focused without distractions during the session.

→ At the end of the timer, take a five-minute rest period.

→ The routine should be repeated four times before taking a break of 15–20 minutes.

Why This Works

→ Short work sessions prevent burnout

→ The knowledge of upcoming breaks helps maintain your drive throughout work sessions.

→ Your brain stays active throughout the period rather than drifting away.

The Pomodoro Technique may be modified by individuals who choose 40-minute work sessions when their attention demands it. Test various approaches to identify the one that works best for you.

How to Prioritize Tasks Without Feeling Overwhelmed

Multiple items on your daily list differ in their level of importance. Task prioritization enables you to concentrate on matters that truly matter.

Ask Yourself These Two Questions:

★ **Is it urgent?** Meaning does it have a near deadline or serious consequences if delayed?

★ **Is it important?** Does it significantly impact your goals, grades, or well-being?

For example:

- **Urgent & Important** → Homework due tomorrow (Do it first!)

- **Important but Not Urgent** → Studying for a test next week (Schedule time for it.)

- **Urgent but Not Important** → Replying to messages about a group project (Handle quickly, but don't let it take over your schedule.)

- **Not Urgent & Not Important** → Watching random YouTube videos (Save it for later!)

OVERCOMING PROCRASTINATION

Regular procrastination develops into constant stress when it turns into an ongoing habit.

The following instructions show how to stop procrastination:

- **The Five-Minute Rule:** You can begin any challenging task by promising yourself to work for just five minutes at first. Starting the work will make continued work feel much simpler.

- **Break Big Tasks into Smaller Steps:** Tasks that are smaller in nature create less stress for the performer, which makes them more approachable to begin.

- **Set Fake Deadlines:** The deadline for your assignment is Wednesday instead of Friday. The practice of setting false deadlines helps your brain to work in advance and avoid late-night stress.

- **Reward Yourself for Finishing Tasks:** You can promise yourself a pleasant reward when you finish a hard task by scheduling a specific entertainment activity, such as watching your favourite show. This builds motivation!

Time operates as your greatest strength in life.

Mastering time management means developing a balanced approach that allows you to work efficiently while maintaining enough leisure time to enjoy your life.

Let's recap the key strategies:

- **Time blocking:** serves as an organizational tool which creates specific periods for each task.

- **The Pomodoro Technique:** Keeps study sessions productive with short breaks.

- **Prioritization:** enables you to concentrate on essential matters while preventing time wastage.

- **Procrastination hacks** enable you to begin work more easily while maintaining your course.

When you gain control over your time, both stress and enjoyment levels in your life will increase significantly.

After mastering time management, we need to discuss organization methods for our lives. The following chapter details the methods for workspace management along with assignment tracking and preventing crucial document losses.

Let's take the next step together!

In the next chapter, we'll break down how to keep track of everything without feeling overwhelmed, so you never have to say, *where did I put that paper? " Or "Wait, when is that test again?*

CHAPTER 3

ORGANIZATION
AND PRIORITIZATION

"Organization isn't about making life boring—
it's about making space for what's exciting."
—Kimberly Myrick

Mia constantly searches for something in her home. Mia's constant search consists of moving from her math notebook to her earbuds until she reaches her gym clothes and finally stops at her charger. As soon as she wakes up, she runs through the house shouting for her missing something.

Mia demonstrates genuine concern about her things. She detests tardiness while seeking to organize herself before anything else. She has never learned fundamental skills about organization and establishing proper priorities. She stays overwhelmed because she struggles to determine her priorities and struggles continuously to play catch-up.

The organization club has a new member who joins right now. Disorder in your life drains your energy while wasting your time and turning your world into an endless search for missing items. The real essence of organization exists beyond achieving perfection in your room setup. Organization involves developing systems that enable you to locate needed items while finishing work tasks efficiently while staying focused on essential matters.

Your ability to organize tasks, along with your talent for intelligent task prioritization, will lead you to exceptional workload management and improved mental peace.

WHY ORGANIZATION AND PRIORITIZATION MATTER

Organization extends beyond basic neatness so it offers many additional advantages beyond simple organization.

People who develop strong organizational abilities benefit from these advantages.

→ You will save time because organized spaces enable you to avoid frantic late-minute scrambles and reduce your search time.

→ A stress-free environment combined with organized scheduling enables better control of your daily responsibilities.

→ The reduction of clutter enables better focus because it prevents unnecessary distractions from occurring.

→ You will not miss important assignments because you keep track of deadlines when you maintain order in your life.

→ Your proactive approach will replace your previous reactive behavior since you will stay ahead of upcoming challenges.

Prioritization enables you to handle your work in the correct sequence. When your essay deadline approaches tomorrow, you will prioritize your work over your desk cleaning duties, which typically take an hour.

Your skill development in these two abilities will protect you from stress and lead to expert-level time management performance.

STEP-BY-STEP GUIDE TO ORGANIZING YOUR SPACE & MATERIALS

Step 1: Organizing Your Physical Space

Your environment greatly affects how well you can concentrate as well as complete tasks effectively. A disorganized backpack, locker or desk will create more challenges for achieving productive work.

Declutter and Take Control

Follow these steps to organize your physical space one by one:

→ Spend five minutes daily before bedtime to organize your environment through the 5-Minute Clean-Up routine. Small efforts prevent big messes.

→ Designate a dedicated storage space for everything to prevent earbud loss. The same goes for school supplies, clothes, and important papers.

→ You should create separate folders with labels for each subject while maintaining them inside your backpack.

→ Once a week during Sunday reset, you should empty your backpack, locker, and desk to prevent clutter accumulation.

A tidy environment produces mental clarity that helps people stay focused while completing their tasks.

Step 2: Organizing Your Digital Life

Digital organization requires the same attention as physical space management because both can become disorganized. The combination of unread emails, disorganized Google Drive files, and scattered files creates a search difficulty for essential items.

How to Declutter Your Digital Life

→ You should create separate folders for your school material, your work documents, and your personal files under the user interface. File names should be descriptive to help you identify them easily.

→ You can use Google Calendar or Notion as your calendar application to manage deadlines and schedule planning together with setting reminders.

→ Unsubscribe from all unnecessary email subscriptions then review your inbox only once per day instead of allowing messages to accumulate.

→ Turn Off Notifications: Too many alerts? Use the mute function to disable notifications from nonessential applications, which will reduce your continuous distractions.

How to Prioritize Like a Pro

When your to-do list contains one million items, which task should you start first?

The "Urgent vs. Important" Rule provides a system to follow:

To manage multiple tasks, you should evaluate each task by asking two questions.

Is it urgent? The task requires immediate attention because it is approaching its deadline.

Is it important? The task needs to create substantial changes to your grades, duties, or health conditions.

→ **Urgent & Important:** Do it now. The urgent task of completing your history paper remains due tomorrow.

→ **Important but Not Urgent:** Schedule it. Example: Studying for a test next week.

→ **Urgent but Not Important:** Handle it quickly. You should handle group project messages as soon as possible.

→ **Not Urgent & Not Important:** Skip it or save it for later. Example: Watching random social media videos.

Using this approach helps you avoid spending your time on unimportant matters.

CREATING A TO-DO LIST THAT WORKS

A bad to-do list can make you feel even more overwhelmed. A good one helps you get things done without stress.

How to Make an Effective To-Do List:

→ The night before writing your list ensures you start every day with direction.

→ When making lists keep the number of items between three and five essential tasks because many tasks become confusing. Prioritize!

→ Large tasks need to be broken down into smaller actionable steps instead of trying to tackle entire research papers directly, focusing on finding three sources, writing an outline then drafting the introduction.

→ Using a planner with checklists enables you to feel motivated by marking off completed tasks.

→ A short, focused to-do list keeps you productive while eliminating overwhelming feelings.

OVERCOMING COMMON ORGANIZATION STRUGGLES

The best organizational systems may not guarantee absolute organizational stability. The following approach helps you overcome typical organizational challenges:

- **I always forget things:** I use sticky notes, phone reminders, or a planner.

- **I start organizing but never keep it up:** Schedule a weekly reset.

- **I don't have time to clean up:** Spend 5 minutes tidying up before bed.

- **I don't know what to prioritize:** Use the Urgent vs. Important rule.

The key is consistency. Small daily habits make a huge difference.

Take Control of Your Time and Space

Creating an organizational system that suits your needs stands above perfection in this process.

→ A clutter-free space: a focused mind.

→ A well-planned schedule: less stress.

→ Smart prioritization: better productivity.

These approaches will provide you with greater control, confidence, and preparedness for any upcoming situations.

Being organized represents merely one aspect of what it takes to win in life.

When distractions, along with notifications and social media, continuously divert your attention from essential matters, what occurs?

We will address this topic in the following section. The next chapter covers focus along with digital distractions, followed by instructions for mental task training.

Do you want to improve your ability to stay focused while reducing distractions?

CHAPTER 4

ENHANCING FOCUS & OVERCOMING DIGITAL DISTRACTIONS

———◆———

"Focus isn't just about paying attention;
it's about ignoring distractions."
— Kimberly Myrick

Devon understands that he needs to concentrate on his studies. His mathematics exam is in 2 days and he promised himself to begin studying in advance. Devon takes a seat at his desk then opens his book followed by his notebook.

But then, his phone buzzes. A simple check of his phone is all he allows himself to do.

Text messages develop into complete verbal exchanges between users. 5 minutes of scrolling begin after receiving a notification.

The memory of a funny video sent by his friend compels him to watch it again. The time passes without notice when he fails to read the first page of his notes and 30 minutes have elapsed.

Panicked, Devon tries to refocus. No more distractions. The sudden entrance of his younger sibling interrupts his study time by asking to borrow his charger. Devon sighs and helps him.

The return to his desk after leaving the room coincides with 10 additional minutes passing by. The session has barely begun yet he feels completely fatigued.

Sound familiar?

Most people experience the struggle of focusing their attention when working because they constantly check their phone and respond to messages while being sidetracked by various random things. Focusing in our current world has become an exceptionally challenging task.

Your brain faces continuous attacks from endless notifications and social media together with constant distractions. Focus functions as a trainable skill comparable to physical muscle development. Learning how to block distractions and enhance your concentration skills will result in increased productivity during shorter working hours without creating extra stress.

Let's break it down.

WHY FOCUS FEELS SO HARD (AND HOW TO FIX IT)

The human brain operates poorly when exposed to today's distracting elements. In previous times we were unaffected by phone alerts and app interruptions and endless content distractions in our work environment. Your brain produces dopamine after every notification since this chemical delivers pleasurable sensations. People find social media scrolling along with video watching more gratifying than homework activities. When you let distractions take control your ability to maintain focus will gradually decrease. The brain adapts to short bursts of entertainment until deep work tasks appear unappealing.

The human brain accepts training that improves focus capabilities.

The key? You need a system.

THE SCIENCE OF DISTRACTION & MULTITASKING

Numerous individuals maintain the belief that their ability to multitask extends to activities such as studying while texting and listening to music while reading or switching between assignments and social media.

The problem? Your brain functions in a manner that prevents it from paying simultaneous attention to multiple activities.

The brain shifts rapidly between different tasks when you try to multitask leading to:

→ Your work pace reduces because it takes you more time to handle each task.

→ Your memory function deteriorates because you become prone to making errors.

→ Your brain ages more quickly when you make continuous task switches because this mental energy drainage occurs.

A Method for Ending Multitasking Behavior While Enhancing Concentration Skills

→ You should use Pomodoro Technique blocks of 25 minutes work followed by 5 minutes break.

→ When you study, activate the Do Not Disturb setting on your phone to disable notifications.

→ Extra tabs remain accessible only when you close them because multiple open tabs increase your risk of distraction.

→ Set your phone to operate in No Distraction mode through a timer challenge that forces you to stay focused for 15 to 30 minutes before letting yourself check social media.

Your work performance and speed will increase when you remove unimportant distractions.

CREATING A STUDY AREA FREE FROM INTERRUPTIONS

Your study environment creates a greater impact on your concentration ability than you probably realize. A disorganized space along with excessive noise or numerous distractions will make it tougher for you to focus

Creating a Focus-Friendly Study Space

→ Select a study space that avoids disturbances by keeping it separate from television areas and loud surroundings and interrupting events.

→ Your work area should only contain necessary materials which you keep in front of yourself.

→ Noise-Cancelling headphones provide an excellent solution to block background noises when you cannot find a quiet place to study.

→ Before beginning your work, establish a specific period when you will refrain from checking your phone.

A focused workspace = a focused mind.

Tame Digital Distractions

Your phone is the #1 focus-killer.

People unconsciously glance at their phones more than 100 times daily. Social media applications together with group messaging systems and alert messages are developed to divert your attention.

Working without phone interruptions requires the following methods

→ Placing your phone in another room will reduce its appeal by increasing distance.

→ The Forest application along with Freedom and Cold Turkey serve as app blockers which lock distracting applications during your work sessions.

→ The system should disable all non-essential alerts because their notifications are unnecessary.

→ Establish specific phone-free study sessions in advance through scheduling.

The amount of time you dedicate to your phone will define your ability to concentrate.

STRENGTHEN YOUR FOCUS MUSCLE

The ability to focus functions similarly to muscles because consistent practice results in enhanced strength.

Concentrating for 15 minutes initially proves challenging to most people. With enough time your brain will develop new habits which enable you to stay focused longer periods without interruptions.

The process of teaching your brain to sustain attention longer

→ Begin with short focus sessions by setting your timer to 10-15 minutes at first and then extend your time later.

→ Intentional breaks should replace continuous work without breaks. A brief five-minute walk or stretch period will help your brain recharge itself.

→ As a strategy to stay engaged you should attempt to finish one additional page or complete one more question or write one more section.

→ Maintain a daily log of your focus duration then aim to extend it with each passing day.

Through regular practice your ability to stay focused will transform into automatic behavior.

Focus functions as your ultimate power in life

Achieving mastery in focus requires more than sheer willpower because it depends on developing proper behavioral patterns and environment conditions.

→ Multitasking activities reduce your overall speed.

→ The area around you determines how productive you will be. Establish a place without distractions.

→ You should manage your phone usage because notifications function as attention-grabbing strategies.

→ You should train your focus ability through tiny beginning steps that grow progressively harder.

Your ability to stay focused will directly improve your productivity while reducing stress levels in your life.

The main issue arises when stress and emotional states take over even if you already maintain good organization and focus.

Our following discussion will show you exactly what to expect. Chapter 5 covers emotional regulation alongside stress management and preserving composure when under pressure.

You are prepared to master emotional control and stress management techniques. Let's find out.

EMOTIONAL REGULATION & STRESS MANAGEMENT

———————◈———————

"Self-control isn't about denying yourself—
it's about choosing what's best for yourself."
—Kimberly Myrick

S ophie demonstrated exceptional abilities as a student. She completed all her work and joined classroom discussions and met every deadline. But lately, things have changed.

She failed her recent math examination a couple of weeks earlier. Her best friend cut off communication without giving any explanation. Her parents applied continuous pressure to her about college applications alongside the other issues she faced. Every trivial matter seemed overwhelming to her.

She spent that afternoon struggling with science quiz preparation when her thoughts raced uncontrollably. What if I fail again? My life would become manageable if my friend started communicating with me again. Will my parents be let down by my actions? She slammed her book shut when her thoughts reached their peak point and left her completely defeated.

Instead of focusing on her studies Sophie picked up her phone to browse social media in order to escape her mounting tension. She checked the time after one hour yet her mood sank lower than when she started. The upcoming quiz remained unattended while stress persisted to haunt her and left her with less preparation time.

Many people experience this situation. Everyone undergoes stress together with frustration and experiences emotional ups and downs. The real issue arises from a person's inability to handle their emotions properly instead of the actual experience of such feelings.

The ability to control emotions together with stress management techniques creates the solution.

Developing skills to handle emotional responses and reduce stress together with remaining collected during crises will unlock transformative changes in your life. And the best part? Anyone can develop it.

WHY EMOTIONAL REGULATION MATTERS

Treat your emotions as if they were a vehicle. When driving if your vehicle encounters slippery ice and you will experience a car skid. Steering wheel control will be lost if you panic by pulling the wheel since this action can cause you to crash. Remaining composed while steering your course will help you recover your control over the situation.

The mechanism for emotional regulation functions identically. A calm state of mind allows you to respond smartly rather than making impulsive reactions when stressful situations happen.

Your ability to control emotions will provide several benefits:

→ Make better decisions, no more reacting out of anger or frustration.

→ You will maintain your composure through adverse situations because you trust your ability to handle problems effectively.

→ You will acquire the ability to stop overthinking along with stress reduction through this practice.

→ Your emotional control will prevent any interruptions from redirecting you from your goals.

Learning to handle emotions leads to a life that becomes simpler to navigate.

RECOGNIZING YOUR EMOTIONAL TRIGGERS

The first step in emotional control demands identification of the triggers that prompt each emotional response.

Consider the most recent occasion when you experienced these feelings:

→ Frustrated – Was it because of schoolwork, family issues, or something else?

→ A poor grade made you feel like you failed according to your emotional state.

→ The feeling of being overwhelmed occurred because you attempted to handle multiple tasks simultaneously.

How to Identify Emotional Triggers

Maintain a journal for stress by noting situations which cause anxiety and frustration together with moments of upset.

→ Your heart starts to race when you experience stress according to your body. Anger triggers you to clench your jaw.

→ Notice your mental processes since you might automatically think of the most negative possible outcome.

→ When you talk to yourself do you ever express negative thoughts toward yourself?

Triggers become simpler to handle once you identify which situations affect you emotionally.

STRESS REDUCTION TECHNIQUES: MINDFULNESS, BREATHING, AND MORE

Stress isn't always bad. A small amount of stress serves as a motivator to complete tasks. The accumulation of stress leads to an overwhelming sensation which results in paralysis.

The following steps will help you manage your stress before stress manages you.

The "Pause and Breathe" Method

Pause your reaction when overwhelming situations occur instead of reacting immediately

→ Pause – Close your eyes for a second.

→ Breathe deeply for four seconds.

→ Hold for four seconds.

→ Exhale slowly for six seconds.

→ Repeat until you feel calmer.

Slowing your breath triggers a signal to your brain which allows it to stop perceiving panic thus enabling clear thinking.

Reframing Negative Thoughts

Your thoughts shape your emotions. Your brain accepts whatever statement you make to yourself so when you say "I'm going to fail this test" stress instantly rises.

Shift your unhelpful negative thoughts by creating balanced replacements.

→ **Negative thoughts** - You will never grasp the material in this subject.

→ **Positive thoughts** - I will get better with practice despite the difficulty of this subject.

→ **Negative thoughts** - **A** failure would create disappointment in all those who count on me.

→ **Positive thoughts** - The single bad grade will not determine who I am. I can recover from this.

→ **Negative thoughts** - I have too much to do. I can't handle it.

→ **Positive thoughts** - To manage the situation I will divide the work into smaller manageable steps while addressing things one by one.

Positive changes to personal dialogue create lower anxiety while building inner conviction.

HEALTHY WAYS TO RELEASE STRESS

When you need to manage your stress, you should consider using different healthy approaches to dealing with difficult situations beyond avoiding emotions or losing yourself to technology.

→ Exercise serves two-fold benefits as it both decreases stress and elevates mood.

→ Soothing music through headphones serves as a mental calming tool.

→ Writing emotions through journaling enables the processing of your feelings.

→ Spend time practicing meditation or deep breathing because they lower the speed of overwhelming thoughts.

→ Drawing, coloring or art projects offer therapeutic benefits, especially when paired with calming music.

Identify which stress-coping methods work best for you and apply them whenever you feel stress approaching.

Building Emotional Resilience

Individuals have different abilities to recover from difficulties as some handle them immediately while others need extended time. The difference? People with emotional resilience maintain their focus under stress while continuing forward.

To develop resilience, you should follow these steps:

You should learn better methods to handle stress rather than trying to avoid it – accept that stress is part of life.

→ Focus on what you can control – Worrying about the past or future wastes energy. Your attention should remain on present actions you can accomplish.

→ Try creating a daily gratitude list which includes three things you appreciate. This approach helps you change your thinking pattern from negative stress toward positive thinking.

→ Seek support from trustworthy people including your family members or mentors if stress becomes too intense.

→ Rather than steering clear from challenges, resilience shows you how to deal with problems while advancing forward.

Your emotions should not rule your life because you possess the power to control them.

Understanding emotional regulation does not ensure complete protection from stress, frustration or anxiety. Through proper learning you will develop healthy methods to deal with your emotions.

→ Examine emotional triggers because this triggers stress or frustration.

→ Try to use breathing techniques together with healthy outlets to effectively manage your stress.

→ Reframe negative thoughts, shift from self-doubt to self-confidence.

→ Your ability to recover from obstacles will increase through developing resilience.

The process of controlling emotions before they take over makes life simpler to handle. You can have excellent emotional control yet still have setbacks and failures, but it's how you handle them that matters. What should you do if circumstances lead you to an unfavorable outcome? That's what we'll tackle next. You will learn to convert setbacks into developmental possibilities and generate unbreakable self-confidence in Chapter 6. Success demands you prepare to transform the way you think about life. Let's find out.

DEVELOPING A GROWTH MINDSET

"Decision-making is easier when your executive functions are strong. Train your brain, transform your life."
—Kimberly Myrick

Since his early years Jordan showed himself to be a rigid perfectionist. During his elementary school years his natural skills created success without requiring much work. His natural achievements created the impression that people have fixed intelligence since they either possess talent or lack it. The difficulties became increasingly harder to overcome when he began high school. A bold red "C" marked on his math test by his teacher caused Jordan to experience a sinking feeling as he thought "I'm completely terrible at math. I'll never understand this." Jordan experienced a deep sense of shock when he saw his classmate Maya's paper which earned an A on the exam compared to his own C grade. Maya provided a simple answer to his question by saying "I also used to have trouble too but with daily practice I began to see improvement."

The response shattered the fundamental belief Jordan had always kept. His belief system based on a fixed mindset made him think that his shortcomings showed his inability to succeed. The growth mindset Maya possessed enabled her to recognize failure as an essential element which leads to better performance. She believed that dedicated work combined with determination enabled her to face any difficulty. The opposing viewpoints about learning would eventually shape Jordan's entire approach to personal development.

The chapter investigates the transformation which occurs when you adopt a growth mindset to handle obstacles because it transforms your dissatisfaction into constructive possibilities. This section teaches you how to rewrite your inner thoughts combined with learning from mistakes while establishing supportive networks for continuous development. Through the course of this book, you will learn failure does not define you, it serves as a temporary stop before making progress and you possess the ability to transform your thinking into positive directions.

What Is a Growth Mindset?

People with growth mindsets believe their abilities and intelligence alongside their skills grow when they commit to work hard while using strategic approaches. The growth mindset stands opposite to fixed mindset beliefs that traits remain unalterable. Individuals with growth mindsets actively face tough situations while staying put in the face of obstacles and understanding setbacks help them gain knowledge.

FIXED MINDSET VS. GROWTH MINDSET

Fixed Mindset:

→ According to this mindset intelligence and talent remain unalterable traits.

→ Views failure as a sign of inherent inability.

→ The person shuns challenges because they fear revealing their vulnerabilities.

→ People with this mindset stop their efforts rapidly when they encounter obstacles.

Growth Mindset:

→ A growth mindset believes that personal abilities become stronger when people dedicate effort along with learning and staying persistent.

→ The individual sees obstacles as chances to enhance their abilities.

→ The learning process naturally includes failure which the individual embraces as an essential part.

➔ The individual demonstrates both persistence and resilience when facing failures.

The red "C" on his math test led Jordan to instantly conclude that he lacked ability in math which demonstrates a fixed mindset. Maya demonstrated the advantages of a growth mindset through her process of improving steadily. This chapter will explain how to develop a growth mindset by overcoming fixed mindset thinking which helps turn your fear of failure into a motivation for growth.

Rewriting Your Inner Voice

Your thoughts inside your head shape both your attitudes and your resulting actions. The brain starts to believe statements that you repeat to yourself when you consistently describe yourself as incapable or when you believe failure defines your identity. The development of a growth mindset requires transforming your internal thoughts.

Flipping the Script

Instead of saying to yourself that math is beyond your abilities you should say to yourself that you haven't mastered this math skill yet and need to practice to become better. Notice the word "yet." A simple word change indicates your current shortcomings will end eventually and improvement remains possible.

Consider these transformations:

→ **Negative** - The previous thought was "I continuously make mistakes."

→ **Positive** - The process of learning helps me grow by examining and learning from all my mistakes.

→ **Negative** - The current challenge seems too big for me.

→ **Positive** - The challenge remains difficult yet dedication will enable me to succeed.

→ **Negative** - Currently my writing abilities fall short.

→ **Positive** - Writing a single word helps my writing improve even though I am not yet a great writer.

You can develop greater resistance through purposeful negative thought conversion that builds internal success messages for positive development. Stop any fixed mindset thought when it occurs and turn it into an affirmative growth-oriented statement. Brain rewiring happens through this method as it teaches you to view difficulties as chances instead of impossible problems.

How to Turn Failures into Learning Opportunities

Mistakes will happen naturally yet each one offers exceptional learning potential. Learning to ride a bicycle demands numerous unsuccessful attempts before mastering the skill of balance. Every mistake provides you with important knowledge to enhance your skills. If you quit instead of picking yourself up after your initial tumble you would have never learned to ride.

❖ **Transforming Failure into Feedback**

After a setback you should ask yourself what lessons you can draw from the situation. The error should not confirm your belief in your incapability; instead, it serves as important guidance for your upcoming attempts.

❖ **Practical Strategies for Learning from Mistakes**

→ **Reflect on the Experience:** Analyzing the situation becomes essential after experiencing a setback. Make a note of your thoughts and emotions and include possible ways to improve. The reflective practice enables people to convert negative results into valuable lessons for improvement.

→ **Celebrate Small Victories:** Acknowledge every minor improvement. All small achievements serve as fundamental elements which strengthen your confidence to advance further.

→ **Separate Your Identity from Your Mistakes:** Your mistakes should not determine the way you see yourself because you are separate from your errors. A mistake should not determine your identity. The mistake serves as a tool to help you progress toward ongoing self-improvement.

→ **Develop a Backup Plan:** You should develop backup plans to handle possible failures in advance. A backup strategy enables relaxation through decreased anxiety and facilitates recovery in case original plans fail to materialize.

The red "C" marked an important lesson for Jordan in math rather than serving as an end to his mathematical journey because it indicated the necessity for additional work. He could transform his learning experience into a pathway to understand academic obstacles as passing challenges which he could master.

The Power of "Yet"

The simple yet powerful word "yet" provides someone with great transformative ability. The addition of yet transforms negative statements into pathways for future success. Your present situation does not define you because you are presently developing into something better.

How "Yet" Transforms Your Mindset

Before: "I can't do this."

After: "I can't do this yet."

The previous state of affairs reflected my inability to deliver speeches effectively.

The public speaking skills which I lack today will improve through continued practice.

Through the word "yet" you can remember that failure exists as a short-term condition while personal development remains always achievable. Your persistence increases because every attempt brings you nearer to mastering yourself. Inserting "yet" into your daily self-dialogue enables you to transition your thinking from being restricted to growing limitless.

CREATING A GROWTH-ORIENTED ENVIRONMENT

Your environment establishes major aspects of how you think. The presence of encouraging people in your environment plays a major role in helping you build a growth mindset.

Cultivating a Supportive Network

- **Select Inspiring Role Models:** Devote time to people who demonstrate growth mindset behavior. Watch how these individuals manage failure as well as how they express their achievements. Their ability to persevere demonstrates to all of us that dedication produces better results.

- **Build Positive Relationships**: Seek relationships with people who push you to succeed through their support. Your social group will strengthen your learning dedication while showing you that difficulties represent chances for growth.

- **Create an Encouraging Environment:** The environment where you find yourself matters so select wholesome locations which encourage both exploration and development whether you stay at home or attend school.

- You should place yourself in environments that contain learning resources such as books and workshops and online courses to spark your desire for improvement.

- **Engage in Constructive Conversations**: Talk about your goals as well as challenges and successes to people who value persistence in their lives. Their suggestions together with their support help you receive essential information which maintains your motivation level.

Establishing an intentional framework for growth leads to the development of a supportive network which reinforces growth mindset development for yourself and motivates every member of your network to continuously improve.

MOVING BEYOND YOUR ESTABLISHED COMFORT BOUNDARIES.

Your development process mostly happens beyond the boundaries of familiar comfort areas. Participating only in familiar areas restricts your potential growth although being there feels secure. A person must step beyond their comfort area to discover fresh abilities and covert capacity.

The Importance of Challenging Yourself

- **New Challenges Foster Growth:** The brain requires adaptation whenever you attempt something unfamiliar. The brain adaptation process enables you to build new capabilities and develops your capability to handle future difficulties effectively.

- **Embrace Discomfort:** Your experience of discomfort when confronting something new will pass in time. Through determined effort what initially seemed intimidating will transform into something controllable while each success will improve your ability to deal with adversity.

- **Expand Your Horizons**: Experiencing novelty through different activities or hobbies leads to encountering new viewpoints and life experiences that develop your understanding of the world at large.

Practical Ways to Challenge Yourself

- **Set Personal Challenges:** Create targeted challenges for the skills or roles that give you doubt such as public speaking or language learning or leadership responsibilities.

- **Take Incremental Risks:** Start with small, low-risk challenges. You should begin by sharing one idea in a group setting but expand your participation level when you gain more self-assurance.

- **Engage in New Experiences:** Take on tasks which differ completely from everything you usually do. Trying something new like clubs, social service or learning an artistic skill enables you to discover more abilities in yourself.

Repeatedly stepping outside your comfort zone helps you establish the mental framework that you possess the ability to transform and develop. Every hurdle presents itself as a means to strengthen your resilience which leads to developing an improved adaptable version of yourself.

GROWTH MINDSET CREATES UNLIMITED ABILITIES

The principles of a growth mindset go beyond just work or school—they're a long-term approach to facing challenges and seizing opportunities in every part of your life. This mindset changes the way you view failure, helping you see it as an important part of growth and personal development. With a growth mindset, every obstacle becomes an opportunity to move closer to your best, most fulfilled self.

Long-Term Benefits of a Growth Mindset

- **Enhanced Learning:** Through embracing challenges your learning speed improves together with the development of new abilities.

- **Improved Problem-Solving**: The practice of turning obstacles into opportunities allows people to develop innovative thinking together with creative solutions.

- **Increased Resilience**: Learning continuously from challenges develops your mental strength which enables you to face adversity in a dignified manner.

- **Self-Motivation:** You will continue making efforts to improve even when progress appears slow because you accept that your work creates results.

- **Holistic Success:** Through a growth mindset people develop success across all life domains including their personal connections and their professional goals.

The way Jordan approached his life reveals that developing a growth mindset represents more than academic enhancement because it becomes a lifeline for personal success. Through embracing challenges along with the learning gained from failure you enhance your potential to discover that success continues as a moving process instead of a fixed destination.

The mindset of growth leads people to build a life dedicated to perpetual betterment.

The math test failure marked a new start for Jordan which launched him into a life-changing expedition. Through his mindset transformation he discovered that each obstacle presents a chance to develop himself. The red "C" mark became an opportunity for him to put in additional effort while discovering innovative approaches to tackle future assignments.

Growth mindset development requires time because it requires changing your self-talk while accepting mistakes and continued commitment to step outside your comfort zone. Developing personal growth demands dedication along with the capacity to use setbacks as educational experiences instead of final capability assessments.

Certain Approaches Help People Develop Their Growth Mindset

- **Rewrite Your Inner Dialogue:** Replace negative thoughts with ones focused on growth and possibility. Shift from saying "I can't do this" to "I can't do this yet," recognizing that challenges are temporary and part of the learning process.

- **Embrace Mistakes:** Each mistake provides you with essential information for development. Review the failed elements to extract knowledge and modify your methods.

- **Surround Yourself with Growth:** Create friendships and find mentors who support persistence while appreciating every learned thing.

- **Step Out of Your Comfort Zone:** Take risks beyond your usual comfort range. Make an effort to try fresh experiences and handle tasks that test your current abilities at least once regularly.

- **Practice Patience and Persistence**: Real growth needs time together with dedication to achieve desired outcomes. Recognize and celebrate minor achievements and continue advancing steadily despite the slowness of results.

  When you implement these practices regularly you will develop strength and determination that turns difficulties into chances for progress. Your growth mindset provides the power to continue learning while growing and achieving thus overcoming any difficulty you encounter.

- ❖ **A Hook to Ignite Your Journey:** You find yourself on the threshold of a new chance with mixed emotions of enthusiasm and doubt. You have transformed your perspective so that failures teach you and challenges guide your progress toward major success.

The same time Jordan realized setbacks offered growth potential you will reach a point that exposes all your assumptions about your potential.

The upcoming obstacle that stands before you might require you to shift your entire life perspective rather than testing your information base. By accepting that challenge you will discover a path to a future in which unlimited growth becomes possible.

The opportunity in front of you is a path to personal discovery and future-focused determination, guiding you step by step toward limitless possibilities. Every challenge you face along the way is a chance to build resilience and bounce back even stronger. The journey of continuous improvement has already begun, and the next chapter holds the breakthroughs that will transform your life.

Through a growth mindset you get ready to achieve academic and professional success yet develop abilities to face life challenges with strength and artistic thinking as well as staunch faith in your abilities. The path of daily challenges develops you into someone who becomes smarter and stronger along with gaining more power.

Now, as you set your sights on the future, ask yourself: How will you harness this newfound resilience to shape the next phase of your journey? Your path is unfolding before you, filled with challenges, growth, and endless opportunities for transformation.

CHAPTER 7

GOAL SETTING
AND ACHIEVEMENT

*"Setting goals without executive functioning skills
is like taking a journey without a map."*
—Kimberly Myrick

The ambitious spirit of Olivia's heart revealed itself clearly through her dreams. From the beginning of her childhood, she made plans to become an agent of transformation. The scope of her aspirations included university admission at a prestigious institution and startup entrepreneurship and international travel. Every fall she wrote down resolutions with a notebook that she thought would lead to her success goals:

→ Study more diligently.

→ Exercise consistently.

→ Save money for future adventures.

→ Write a book someday.

→ Learn a new language.

→ Build a network of mentors.

The process of goal-setting briefly gave her a feeling of omnipotence. Time turned out to be a powerful eraser that removed the initial excitement. During the second month of her resolutions half of them vanished completely while the remaining ones burned out rather than sustaining her through time. During those few days when she focused on studying, she would lose concentration because social gatherings spoke to her or creative activities grabbed her attention or she yielded to procrastination. Deadlines created stacks of work which caused her exercise plan to fade away. The mix of exhilaration and annoying unreachability characterized Olivia's pursuit of her goals.

Her failure stemmed from not having a well-defined path to follow and sustaining forward progress. Through her experiences Olivia discovered that setting goals cannot be done by wishing or being lucky. This ability requires training because it functions as a process which needs appropriate methods and mental approach to reach mastery. The following section will show you how to change aspirations into practicable steps through which your ambitions will transform into concrete results.

Why Goal Setting Matters

Life can feel aimless when you don't have clear goals, like wandering through an endless maze with no way out. Setting personal goals gives you a roadmap, helping you focus on what truly matters and stay driven. When you set realistic goals, you create milestones to track your progress, which not only keeps you motivated but also shows you how far you've come.

Benefits of Effective Goal Setting

Define your goals precisely because this helps you maintain constant awareness of your work priorities. Your decisions and actions always support the big picture goals which allows you to stay focused and regulated.

- **Clarity and Focus:** Small milestone achievements create stronger motivation because they deliver satisfaction to your morale. Moving ahead in life brings joy since it demonstrates continuous progress toward your dreams.

- **Enhanced Motivation:** By monitoring what you accomplish you gain the ability to measure accurately how much you have grown. The feedback process strengthens your dedication as it enables you to redirect your actions whenever necessary.

- **Measurable Progress:** Setting and reaching objectives teaches you to develop self-control through consistent practice. Through the process you will develop personal discipline which eventually transforms into a vital success factor.

The understanding of these advantages creates the essential basis for why learning goal setting methods extends beyond classroom studies because it develops into a fundamental skill which directs your life's path.

SETTING SMART GOALS FOR LONG-TERM SUCCESS

The main challenge in goal setting appears when people make their goals too general or too vague. The goal of wanting improved math skills remains commendable yet lacks sufficient detail for effective implementation. The solution? A goal setting process called the SMART formula results in well-defined practical objectives out of ordinary aspirations.

Breaking Down SMART Goals

- **Specific:** The goal needs to be precise through a definitive description of your desired outcome. Focus on a specific area of math combined with exact skills for improvement instead of simply wanting to become better at math.

- **Measurable:** Establish criteria for tracking progress. Your goals should specify both a specific test score alongside a fixed number of practice problems to master.

- **Achievable:** Your goal should be difficult to reach but not too difficult that it's unattainable. The goal must stretch your capabilities but at the same time remain attainable through your dedicated work.

- **Relevant:** Your goal must have direct connections to your future ambitions and life dreams. The individual targets you set need to connect to your ultimate vision for development.

- **Time-bound:** Establish a timeframe to establish a feeling of urgency. The knowledge of your time limit helps you stay focused on steady development toward your objective.

An Example in Practice

The goal of Olivia who wants to better her math abilities serves as an example. A goal statement which begins with "I want to improve in math" can evolve into the SMART goal: "I will study algebra for 30 minutes daily during the next 12-weeks aiming for at least 15% better test results."

SMART Version: The SMART goal states that I will dedicate 30 minutes each day for algebra study during the next 12 weeks and hope to raise my test scores by minimum 15% when the term ends.

This updated objective presents algebra as its specific subject while providing measurable quantities of 30 minutes daily study time and 15% score improvement and demonstrates achievable results through dedicated work and maintains direct connection to her academic goals within a 12-week timeframe. The formula produces goals which become both clear and manageable thus enabling easier creation of plans.

BREAKING BIG GOALS INTO SMALLER STEPS

Large goals can be overwhelming. The entire book project or business startup appears impossible when considered as one big project instead of multiple smaller steps. Transforming enormous goals into manageable smaller steps represents the solution for success.

How to Deconstruct a Big Goal

Olivia wants to write a 50,000-word book which represents her writing dream. A single large approach to the project creates conditions that cause both procrastination and burnout to occur. She transforms the project into step-by-step operational procedures.

- **Outline the Book:** The first step includes creating a thorough outline for both chapters and main concepts.

- **Set Daily Writing Targets:** People who want to write daily should establish themselves to produce 500 words per day.

- **Create a Timeline for the First Draft:** Develop a schedule for drafting the first version to finish it in twelve weeks.

- **Plan the Editing Process:** The editing process should follow a weekly schedule where each chapter gets dedicated one week for complete revisions.

- **Prepare for Publication:** After reaching manuscript perfection it is advisable to let trusted peers or professional editors review the work.

Breaking a big goal into smaller, more manageable parts turns each achievement into a milestone that feels easy to reach. This approach helps prevent that overwhelming feeling and keeps you focused. By tackling one step at a time, you create steady progress, maintaining momentum and ensuring you don't lose sight of your goals along the way.

OVERCOMING PROCRASTINATION AND STAYING CONSISTENT

Even the best plans can be thrown off track by procrastination, which can be one of the biggest obstacles to progress. A lot of people have experienced the pattern of starting out strong and motivated, only to follow up with long periods of inaction. Olivia was no exception to this—she often found herself working intensely for short bursts, only to wait for extended periods before diving back into the task. This cycle can be frustrating and slow down your progress, but it's not impossible to break. By using specific strategies to minimize procrastination and create consistent routines, you can shift away from this pattern and start making steady progress toward your goals.

Strategies to Combat Procrastination

- **The 5-Minute Rule:** Begin by dedicating yourself to work on your task for only five minutes under the 5-Minute Rule. The short amount of time required for this commitment frequently helps you break through initial delays to start working and allows progress after the initial start.

- **Accountability Partners:** The support of accountability partners involves revealing your goals to someone who will maintain your progress through regular check-ins. You will maintain your progress as long-term goals by establishing regular check-ins which provide the necessary gentle pressure.

- **Visual Reminders:** You should utilize vision boards and digital alerts together with sticky notes to maintain your goals in full view. Consistent visual reminders throughout your environment act to keep your promises in front of your mind.

- **Progress Tracking:** Track your daily progress through journaling or by using habit tracker apps. You should commemorate your small accomplishments to build up your motivation for continued success.

- **Structured Routines:** People should schedule specific periods for their goal-oriented tasks. The establishment of steady routines eventually turns into an automatic pattern because consistent patterns lead to predictable results.

These tactics establish a system that makes both starting new tasks and maintaining consistency easier to achieve. With continual practice the habit to complete tasks builds up until procrastination becomes less appealing.

The real force behind your persistence between motivation and discipline

Motivation serves as a strong force which drives people during the first phase of their objectives. The fresh start generates enough enthusiasm to stimulate your movement forward. The power of motivation exists only briefly before disappearing completely. Progress depends on discipline because it enables you to push forward despite lacking inspiration.

Understanding the Balance

- **Motivation:** The spark which starts your journey is called motivation. The feeling of enthusiasm arises which prepares you to confront your challenges. Motivation shows changes according to how emotions and situations and external factors influence you.

- **Discipline:** The reliability of discipline enables you to maintain progression throughout all circumstances.

Self-discipline works through routine habits which let objectives advance smoothly even during times when motivation drops off.

Building Self-Discipline

- **Create a Consistent Routine:** Build a regular plan by including your goal-related duties in your daily tasks. Creating a set schedule saves energy by decreasing the number of decisions you need to make along with improving your ability to stay focused.

- **Eliminate Distractions:** Identify distractions including phone usage and loud settings after which you should create efficient strategies to reduce them.

- **Set Milestone Rewards:** Establish specific awards for yourself when you reach your different intermediate goals. The rewards you give yourself need not be expensive since brief rest periods along with preferred snacks or leisure moments will strengthen your dedication.

- **Visualize the End Goal:** Your end goal success remains visible through continual mental focus. Review the original purpose of your goal and envision how the achievement will make you feel and change your life.

- **Check Your Progress:** Regularly review your progress and assess your current approach to identify areas for improvement. Self-reflection helps you see what's working well and what isn't, giving you the chance to adjust your strategy and get better results moving forward.

Building discipline is what creates resilience, and that resilience protects your progress from relying solely on short bursts of motivation. Motivation can be unpredictable, but discipline keeps you moving forward, even when motivation fades. Successful people understand this, and they show up day after day, no matter how they're feeling or what's going on around them. Their commitment doesn't depend on their mood or external circumstances—it's built into their routine, and they stay consistent no matter what challenges come their way.

TRACKING PROGRESS & ADAPTING WHEN THINGS GO WRONG

Every successful journey is filled with setbacks along the way. Even the best strategies can't protect you from obstacles, missed deadlines, or moments when you feel discouraged. These bumps in the road are a normal part of the process. The key is not to let them define your overall journey. Instead, view them as opportunities to learn, grow, and refine your approach. With each setback, you get better at handling challenges and adjusting your plans to keep moving forward.

Strategies for Bouncing Back

- **Forgive Yourself:** Knowing that one missed day or falling behind schedule does not equal failure. Give yourself some grace. Do not let setbacks turn into discouragement; you need to practice self-forgiveness.

- **Analyze and Learn:** Take some time to reflect on what caused the setback. It might have happened because you got sidetracked, set too many goals at once, or didn't plan your time well. By figuring out what went wrong, you can adjust your plan and set yourself up for better results next time.

- **Adjust Your Approach:** Be willing to adjust your approach when certain strategies aren't working. If things aren't going as planned, tweak your schedule, rethink your goals, and don't hesitate to ask others for advice or guidance.

- **Keep the Long-Term Vision in Focus:** Remember your future aspirations together with their fundamental reasons for your goals. Your strategic view of the situation will restore your strength and clarity to keep moving forward during times of setback.

- **Celebrate Recovery:** Each time you conquer a setback you should dedicate time to appreciate your recovery power. Self-recognition of recovery strength creates optimism which leads to future challenge success.

Every path includes obstacles which you should expect to encounter along the way. Failure serves as a fundamental lesson which shows that it leads people toward their ultimate success.

Additional Strategies for Goal Setting Success

The following additional steps will help you maximize your goal-setting process when combined with the fundamental steps previously described:

- **Prioritize Your Goals:** Having multiple goals requires you to establish priorities among them. Determine which objectives correspond best to your future plans and which ones will produce the most significant effects on your existence. Choosing several essential goals enables you to reduce mental overload so that you direct your resources toward the most pressing matters.

- **Create a Vision Board:** Using visual representations of your goals will provide you with effective motivation for reaching them. Using either a traditional board in your living space or a virtual collection on your digital device allows you to create vision boards which display both your future targets and their significant value.

- **Use Positive Affirmations:** Your belief in your capability to reach success increases through positive thoughts that you speak to yourself. Establish positive affirmations which represent your personal strengths together with your targeted objectives then practice them often. With regular repetition of positive statements, they will create the self-confidence needed to maintain goal success.

- **Keep a Success Journal:** Write down your accomplishments alongside the knowledge gained when dealing with obstacles. A success journal functions as both an achievement record system and motivational aid to help you stay motivated during low points.

- **Seek Guidance and Mentorship:** Educational knowledge received from people who have walked this path before remains a valuable source of wisdom. Teachers, coaches and mentors who achieved their targets will help support your accomplishments through their valuable knowledge and serve to maintain both your accountability and motivation.

- **Embrace a Growth Mindset:** Your capabilities will improve through continuous effort because of your persistence. Those who adopt growth mindsets turn their obstacles into learning opportunities. The mindset functions as a foundation to preserve discipline and resilience during the extensive period.

Growth mindset creates a life of continuous improvement

Goal setting success requires deliberate planning and clear objectives alongside strong commitment and needs regular improvement. Olivia proves that dreams achieve reality by turning them into actionable goals. The guidance in this chapter shows people how to make successful goal setting tools that produce success plans.

Let's recap the key takeaways:

- **SMART Goals:** To qualify as an effective goal, it needs to satisfy all criteria from the SMART principles including Specificity, Measurability, Achievability, Relevancy and Time-Based constraints. You will develop specific goals from unclear desires by using this approach.

- **Break It Down:** The process of dividing large goals into smaller sequential parts enables their achievement. A goal sequence operates as distinct elements that move progressively toward reaching the ultimate target.

- **Combat Procrastination:** Three strategies that help people overcome procrastination include five-minute rules alongside partner accountability systems and visual tracking mechanisms. Continuous small steps lead to the development of consistency.

- **Discipline Over Motivation:** Your path needs discipline more than motivation because motivation starts your journey but discipline sustains you until the end. Develop routines that reduce distractions while rewarding yourself when you maintain consistency in your habits.

- **Learn from Setbacks:** Use setbacks as chances to gain knowledge which helps you move forward. Examine the failures to find their causes then adapt your plan while maintaining your long-term objectives. Every failure presents you with an opportunity to make yourself tougher.

- **Supplement with Additional Strategies:** You can enhance your success journey by giving your goals priority, creating vision boards, using affirmations and obtaining mentorship.

The process of transforming your goals into concrete achievements goes beyond identifying annual goals at the first month of the year. Creating this dynamic system means developing an approach that follows your changes and indicates support while continuously helping you become the best version of yourself. The strategies outlined in this chapter equip you with the tools you need to stay focused and push through challenges. Whether you're aiming for long-term success in life, excelling in school, building a startup, or chasing your personal dreams, these methods will help you stay on track and keep moving forward. By using these techniques, you'll be able to overcome setbacks and work toward your goals with determination and confidence.

Olivia started out with big goals, but she quickly realized she wasn't keeping up with most of her resolutions. It wasn't until she created a solid plan and stuck to it that she was able to push through challenges and move closer to her dreams. And you can do the same. Achieving your goals isn't just about the end result; it's about focusing on both the process and the outcome. Every small step forward helps you build your future and grow stronger along the way.

Now, to take your goal-setting to the next level, you'll need to work on how you communicate and collaborate with others. Chapter 8 dives into communication and teamwork skills that will boost your chances of success. Being a great communicator is something you can learn and improve on—it's in your control.

By using these strategies and developing the right mindset, you can turn simple resolutions into real achievements. Staying on track throughout a long journey takes discipline and perseverance, but if you take it step by step, you'll get closer to your dream goals.

CHAPTER 8

COMMUNICATION AND COLLABORATION

—◆—

"Improving executive functioning skills is like upgrading your mental software—it helps everything run smoother."
—Kimberely Myrick

E than represents the common experience of people who avoid expressing themselves in public environments

The loud rhythm of his heartbeat made Ethan unable to hear the teacher's words as he sat in his classroom. The student crossed his fingers and hoped to stay unselected. "Please don't pick me." Public speaking acted as a psychological edge of a cliff to him. His expertise in the subject did not stop his voice from shaking while his mind became empty and his ideas fell into disarray during speech delivery.

The same difficulty continued to affect him during group work assignments. Ethan spent most of his time observing from the background because he preferred to stay quiet to prevent disagreements. The disagreements made him avoid conversation because he believed quietness would help preserve the peace. His concern about appearing inadequate as well as unprepared prevented him from seeking help even when he needed it. Ethan faces the same type of anxiety as numerous others because his fear of being judged and his overwhelming performance anxiety surpasses his intellectual capabilities.

Most people have experienced both nervousness about speaking their minds and difficulty voicing themselves during group conversations. Communication represents an ability that people can learn through strategic methods and deliberate personal development.

Why Communication Matters

Communication exists beyond verbal speech because it teaches you to share messages precisely and receive messages from others to establish genuine interpersonal bonds. Creating trust-based success together with others depends on effective communication both in personal and professional domains.

The Benefits of Strong Communication Skills

- **Confidence in Expression:** Expressing ideas articulately enables you to develop self-assurance as a person. The built-up confidence eventually serves as a base that supports your personal development together with your professional advancement.

- **Conflict Resolution:** The ability to communicate effectively will provide you with resolution methods that convert conflicts into constructive situations where people understand each other better.

- **Team Collaboration:** Team Collaboration benefits from strong communication since it helps teams listen to each member and unify their shared work efforts.

- **Self-Advocacy:** Clear self-expression of your needs leads to obtaining both support and necessary opportunities you deserve. Self-advocacy stands as an essential process when you seek support in any personal matter.

- **Relationship Building:** Relationships become stronger by using compassionate communication which helps develop sustainable bond formation between people.

Learning these skills builds a strong connection and trust, helping you succeed in every area of your life.

HOW TO EXPRESS YOURSELF CLEARLY & CONFIDENTLY

Ethan and numerous others hold back from expressing themselves because they worry about both judgment and mistakes. Practice dedicated learning will lead to the development of clear and confident expression abilities.

Strategies to Express Yourself Clearly

- **Pause and Organize Your Thoughts:** Take a brief period of time before speaking to organize your thoughts. Taking a short break allows you to arrange your ideas properly while minimizing verbal errors during speech.

- **Use Simple, Direct Language:** Clarity is key. The message will be easier to understand through simple language which removes technical jargon and complex explanations.

- **Maintain Eye Contact:** Making eye contact establishes both engagement between you and others along with a perception of self-confidence. Using eye contact during communication enables you to build trust with your audience while increasing your self-assurance at the same time.

- **Speak at a Steady Pace:** Quick speech causes your audience to become confused. Your ideas will reach listeners better when you maintain a controlled speaking speed.

- **Practice Aloud:** Presentations and important points require practice by standing in front of either a mirror or a supportive friend. Regular practice of your material creates both comfort with your content and anxiety reduction when you speak in front of others.

- **Adopt a Positive Posture:** Position your body with your shoulders straight and your head elevated. When you maintain a confident posture, it strengthens what you say while simultaneously improving your self-confidence.

Ethan began his path toward speaking up through the execution of deliberate small steps. He developed his courage to participate in class by practicing in secure environments before sharing his thoughts with his classmates.

ACTIVE LISTENING AND HANDLING CONFLICT

Listening in an active manner holds equal importance to the typical understanding of effective communication through speaking. The practice requires complete attention to the speaker combined with information processing and deliberate responses which leads to better relationships and deeper understanding.

How to Become an Active Listener

- **Give Your Full Attention:** Devote your complete attention to the speaker by putting your phone away and closing all open tabs from your screen. The behavior demonstrates both appreciation and sincere curiosity for the speaker.

- **Use Positive Body Language:** Forward leaning chest posture combined with eye contact and nodding demonstrates to others that you actively listen to what they say.

- **Paraphrase and Reflect:** When you have understood what the speaker communicated you can state it back through expressions such as "So what you're saying is…" This verification approach shows that you comprehend the information while enabling both parties to clarify any points.

- **Ask Open-Ended Questions:** Open up conversation flow by asking questions which need more than a basic agreement or disagreement. Your active listening skills become more profound because it reveals your genuine interest in the speaker's point of view.

- **Avoid Interrupting:** The speaker needs time to complete their point before you initiate your response. The flow of conversation gets disrupted when someone interrupts and this creates a sense of undervaluation in the speaker.

- **Practice Empathy:** You should make an effort to grasp the emotions and thoughts expressed by the person speaking. Through empathetic listening people develop trust which produces a space where all members feel respected and heard.

Active listening creates transformative conversations because it guarantees that every person involved feels respected which produces more productive and meaningful dialogues.

HOW TO HANDLE CONFLICT

Life brings unavoidable conflict which we all encounter. Handling disagreements with friends and groupmates will either create damaging tensions or beneficial growth opportunities.

Techniques for Resolving Conflict Effectively

- **Stay Calm and Centered:** When emotional situations happen, take a deep breath to achieve inner tranquility. Conflicts benefit from a clear mind that emerges from staying calm.

- **Keep your focus on the issue rather than directing your words at the person involved:** Your frustration needs a direct explanation instead of directing it toward individuals. The objective method directs discussion toward identifying solutions.

- **Use "I" Statements:** Present your current emotional state using statements that do not accuse or blame others. Using "I feel frustrated when" provides a way to share your personal experiences in a manner that stops your conversation partner from becoming defensive.

- **Seek to Understand Before Responding:** Complete understanding of their perspective allows you to formulate your thoughts before expressing them. The discovery of mutual agreement points between both parties' results from learning each other's position.

- **Agree on a Way Forward:** The group must unite to find responses that meet all needs. Every participant might need to surrender personal demands to find solutions which meet their needs.

- **Identifying the appropriate moment to conclude the discussion represents a vital factor:** Continuing with the discussion becomes unnecessary when emotions get out of control since waiting for a later time will generate better results. Short breaks enable situations to calm down and offer thinking time.

Ethan learned from the experience that constructive conflict resolution techniques allowed people to understand each other better and build stronger relationships. He understood conflict differently and to make it an instrument that helps solve misunderstandings by fostering mutual respect instead of seeking to avoid conflicts.

EFFECTIVE GROUP AND TEAM COLLABORATION METHODS

The requirement for teamwork exists in academic settings as well as in professional work environments. The process of working in groups becomes difficult when members exhibit different work ethics and communication approaches. Successful collaboration depends entirely on effective teamwork as its fundamental element.

Strategies for Effective Teamwork

- **Establish Clear Roles and Responsibilities:** Every group project needs to establish clear assignments for team members at its beginning. When roles exist clearly the team avoids misunderstandings while maintaining complete task coverage.

- **Set Shared Team Goals:** The project objective should be defined as a whole then divided into multiple operational steps. The unified perspective maintains both focus and team motivation.

- **Encourage Open Communication:** Establish an environment which provides security for team members to exchange their thoughts and opinions freely. The establishment of regular meetings together with open discussions helps in this process.

- **Leverage Individual Strengths:** Team members should work together to acknowledge their individual capabilities so these strengths can be used to achieve project goals. A team achieves better balance and performance through task distribution based on member competence levels.

- **Hold Each Other Accountable:** A tracking system must be developed alongside procedures to address any problems which arise. Routine check-ins provide the team with opportunities to monitor member contributions and solve emerging problems swiftly.

- **Celebrate Collective Successes:** The team deserves recognition for each accomplishment regardless of its size. The positive team dynamic strengthens through these actions which motivates the team members to continue working together.

Group projects that function well allow members to combine their efforts so their collective work becomes stronger than what any single person could produce independently.

Asking for help and taking personal action to defend your needs.

The fear of appearing weak or burdensome prevents numerous people from requesting help. Success together with personal development requires the ability to identify appropriate times to request help which forms an essential skill for self-advocacy

Tips for Asking for Help Confidently

- **Be Direct and Specific:** Clearly articulate what you need. Instead of expressing confusion, state that you require guidance to understand the concept better.

- **Select your help request period along with the suitable environment:** Seek the perfect moment to request assistance from someone who is not preoccupied with other tasks or responsibilities. A proper environment which shows respect will boost the chances of getting a helpful response.

- **Explain Why You Need Help:** The understanding of your situation will drive others to support your needs. The statement "This project demands I receive help because it determines my final grade" effectively shows why you require assistance.

- **Start Small:** Begin by requesting assistance in situations where the outcome does not affect your performance to increase your comfort level. Regular practice of seeking help will eventually enable you to confront larger challenges with greater ease.

- **Reframe Help-Seeking as a Strength:** Seeking help demonstrates proactive learning behavior rather than demonstrating weakness in any way. Multiple accomplished people credit their accomplishments to their ability to recognize assistance opportunities.

- **Self-advocacy:** It transforms obstacles into opportunities. Your growth and success will improve through the development of support networks which you create when you ask for help with confidence.

- **Enhancing Communication Beyond Words:** Communication goes well beyond what we express through words. Three primary communication methods which influence human relationships include nonverbal cues, written correspondence and digital interactions.

- **The Role of Nonverbal Communication:** Physical behaviors together with facial expressions and body movements frequently express emotions that surpass verbal messages.

To enhance your overall communication.

- **Maintain Good Posture:** Your posture should remain upright whenever you stand or sit to express confidence.

Your message can gain emphasis through proper use of hand movements together with nodding gestures.

- **Align Facial Expressions:** Face expressions should remain in line with verbal statements to prevent creating contradictory body language signals.

Your nonverbal signals together with verbal communication strengthen the way you connect with your audience.

Digital Communication Skills

The modern digital environment leads most people to interact through online channels. Online communication through email together with messaging apps and social media demands clear digital correspondence.

→ Start all digital communications with direct and concise statements when preparing messages or emails. Clarity prevents misunderstandings.

→ Online interactions require a professional tone because it enhances your credibility even when discussing casual matters.

→ You demonstrate both time sensitivity and conversation importance through quick response times.

→ Digital Etiquette practice requires you to select proper language with correct formatting while using emojis correctly to maintain message interpretation.

When you master both nonverbal communication and digital communication your interactive abilities will expand which makes you more successful at communication in all situations.

Collaborative Techniques for Effective Communication

Successful teamwork demands go beyond individual communication competencies by requiring group members to cooperate while exchanging thoughts to discover shared ground. The following collaborative methods will improve team communication:

- **Brainstorming Sessions:** When multiple people participate in group brainstorming, they solve problems more creatively while creating numerous distinct ideas.

- **Create a Safe Space:** To conduct an effective session each team member needs a secure atmosphere to share their thoughts without facing criticism.

- **Encourage Ideas:** At the beginning stage prioritize gathering a vast number of ideas while setting aside the evaluation of their quality. Every idea is welcome.

- **Organize and Prioritize:** Team members should work together to transform the collected ideas into operational plans after they have been presented.

- **Group Decision-Making:** Group decision-making becomes essential for teams to reach their collective objectives.

- **Establish Clear Criteria:** The team should establish specific success indicators to help members evaluate options in an unbiased manner.

- **Facilitate Inclusive Discussion:** The discussion should include all voices through a structured format or by giving each participant time to speak.

- **Reach a Consensus:** Communicate to find a decision which every team member will endorse regardless of their initial preferences. The achievement of team success depends on members learning to compromise with one another.

- **Conflict Resolution Within Teams:** Even well-functioning teams encounter conflicts. Successful resolution of such problems becomes essential for team success

- **Clear Rules:** Teams must establish specific rules about respectful communication together with proper conduct standards.

- **Mediate Impartially:** During conflicts you should first listen to all involved parties before you present any solutions.

- **Focus on Actionable Solutions:** Teams should search for practical solutions which solve problems instead of staying focused on problems.

- **Avoiding heated situations:** This can produce beneficial results since people gain perspective after taking time to calm down.

Teams that implement these collaborative approaches can improve their teamwork while maximizing individual member capabilities to reach their common targets.

Building Your Communication Action Plan

The continuous development of communication abilities with collaboration skills remains a permanent process. The step-by-step creation of an action plan helps you include these abilities in your everyday activities.

Steps to Create Your Communication Action Plan

- **Self-Assessment:** Evaluate how you currently communicate with others. Determine which situations lead to your success while also determining which aspects require development. Maintain a journal as a record of your communication achievements.

- **Set Specific Communication Goals:** Establish your communication objectives by following the SMART goal model. My goal is to start meaningful talks once a week with teachers and peers throughout three months to develop my public speaking abilities.

- **Commit to Active Listening:** Actively listen to others in every single conversation you have. Rephrase the statements of others before asking questions to confirm understanding.

- **Develop a Public Speaking Routine:** The path to conquering your speaking apprehension begins with participation in small group discussions or membership at Toastmasters public speaking clubs. Work your way through speaking opportunities that have minimal pressure until you reach comfort levels with groups of all sizes.

- **Engage in Role-Playing:** Perform several simulated communication drills about requesting assistance while also handling disputes with a friend or mentor. Role-playing helps you become less anxious through experience with multiple situations.

- **Seek Feedback Regularly:** When completing demanding communication tasks request useful feedback from peers and teachers. Such practice will help you develop better techniques while also increasing your communication comfort during the learning process.

- **Incorporate Nonverbal and Digital Strategies:** The integration of physical signals with spoken messages should become your habit while your digital content needs to maintain professional clarity. These abilities will automatically occur through practice over time.

- **Review and Adjust Your Plan:** Periodically assess your progress. Use appreciation of achievements together with lessons learned from failure to modify your course of action for steady improvement.

These steps enable you to develop new communication routines which will turn each interaction into a learning experience.

Communication as Your Superpower

The fear of expressing yourself prevents you from reaching your complete potential according to Ethan's experience. Success depends on strong communication together with collaborative work whether one interacts in school or professional workplaces or personal circles. After mastering these skills you will gain access to richer connections and creative thoughts that lead to various prospects.

Mastering communication requires completing four essential steps defined below.

→ Development work repeatedly combined with proper posture and controlled delivery timing gives you the ability to conquer your stage fright when speaking publicly.

→ Engaging fully through active listening means removing distractions and summarizing others' points followed by thoughtful questions which builds trust and understanding between people.

→ Conflict Resolution techniques that embrace "I" statements allow solving problems without blame which produces beneficial growth opportunities from disagreements.

→ Added to productive teamwork is defining responsibilities and establishing common goals with team members while celebrating every team success together.

→ Personal and professional development requires the ability to both seek assistance and defend your requirements through self-advocacy.

Each skill you enhance moves you nearer to achieving your maximum abilities. Your strategic implementation will lead to better personal connection and productive collaboration while enhancing your relationships with others in your life. The moment you gain control over these fundamental abilities a fresh complicated situation emerges before you. The perfect scenario unfolds when your communication remains unambiguous while your team functions smoothly alongside your self-advocacy which brings fantastic chances through open doors. An unexpected crisis suddenly appears to challenge your capacities for speaking up combined with team collaboration as well as leadership abilities in such difficult times.

Major project failures and personal conflicts that get out of hand present significant challenges to your ability to function in such situations. Each interaction will become a dangerous situation now that everything is at its highest risk point so can you trust the abilities that took you long to master? The genuine assessment of your communication abilities begins now because you enter unfamiliar professional terrain.

In the next chapter, we'll dive into how to adapt to change and build resilience—skills you'll need to tackle unexpected challenges just as effectively as you've learned to handle others. Right now, it's important to start preparing yourself to reclaim your power when life throws curveballs your way.

The lessons in this chapter have given you the tools to master communication and collaboration. You're at a new stage in your journey, equipped with the skills to express yourself clearly, listen actively, resolve conflicts, and work well with others. But with change on the horizon, one crucial question remains:

When the calm period ends, you'll face challenges that demand skills you might not have yet developed. These upcoming tests could push you to rethink how you respond to the unexpected. Are you ready to face what comes next?

CHAPTER 9

ADAPTING TO CHANGE AND BUILDING RESILIENCE

---◈---

"Executive function skills are critical for school success, emotional resilience, and achieving life goals."
— *Russell A. Barkley,*

Planning was a natural habit for Ava throughout her life. Before starting her day, she woke up at 6:30 AM to jog followed by a healthy, brain-balanced breakfast before arriving early to school. Every day followed a precise schedule which gave her both comfort and the ability to predict what lay ahead. The unexpected arrival of that day transformed everything.

Her parents revealed that evening that their family would relocate to an unfamiliar urban area. The upcoming move to a different school delivered an abrupt end to her familiar daily pattern which replaced her regular routine with unknown territory. The breaking news hit her like a powerful wind storm which broke all the precise arrangements she had made for her schedule.

Initially Ava attempted to comfort herself with the thought that she always adjusted to changes in the past. When the new academic year dawned, she began feeling anxious because she wondered whether she would establish friendships. The thought of failing to maintain my academic performance causes me deep concern. Will I develop a strong dislike toward this unfamiliar place? The spirited cafeteria overwhelmed her when she entered her first day at school because she couldn't find anyone familiar nor an unclaimed seat among the laughing groups that already formed their cliques.

All who have gone through abrupt changes like moving or school transfers or relationship losses or major difficulties understand the overwhelming emotional reaction which follows. Change creates feelings of intimidation and frustration while also inducing paralysis in people. Each transformation brings the prospect of personal growth underneath its surface. Your actual adaptability surpasses everything you believe about yourself.

The chapter investigates methods to handle change along with recovery techniques from obstacles and development of personal resilience. The correct strategies combined with a growth-oriented mindset will transform unpredictable life events into growth opportunities that strengthen your wisdom.

WHY CHANGE FEELS DIFFICULT (AND HOW TO MAKE IT EASIER)

Our brains naturally prefer stability and predictability. Routines make us feel safe. When unexpected changes happen, our brains often see them as threats, which can lead to stress and anxiety. These reactions can make us feel overwhelmed and stuck. But the good news? You can train yourself to be more adaptable.

Accepting change is a part of life, and learning to go with the flow helps you build the skills to adjust. By embracing new experiences and letting go of things that no longer serve you, you can navigate life's changes with more ease.

The first step is to recognize that change is an unavoidable part of life. It's something we can't control, but we can control how we respond to it. The key to adapting to change is learning to accept it. Change is always happening, and it's a fundamental truth of life. Think about all the changes you've already faced—advancing to higher grade levels, making new friends, or mastering new skills. Each of those times required you to adjust, to step out of your comfort zone, and to embrace something new. And guess what? You've come through it all successfully. This shows that you have the ability to adapt, even when things feel uncertain.

Embracing Change: Practical Strategies

- **Acknowledge Your Emotions:** Change creates natural emotional responses that include anxiety together with sadness and occasional anger. Accept your emotions even though you should do so without self-criticism. Writing your emotions within a journal or sharing them with someone you trust will help you find emotional release.

- **Your attention should remain on what you actually hold authority to manage:** Although you cannot alter the upcoming change you retain authority over how you react to it. Before moving to a new city take the lead to study the area and discover its events while establishing thrilling personal goals. Controlling your energy toward manageable tasks helps you rebuild your sense of control.

- **Reflect on Past Successes:** Go back in your memory to recall past changes you handled successfully. Transitions to new classes and personal wins are among the achievements that helped you adapt well to change. The recollection of these experiences reminds you about your personal strength and strengthens your belief in your future ability to adjust to new situations.

- **Visualize a Positive Outcome:** You should direct your attention toward the beneficial changes instead of worrying about possible disadvantages. New relationships with people along with distinctive experiences and individual development opportunities will become part of your future. A single visualization practice allows you to transition fear into optimistic anticipation.

Using these strategies along with accepting natural life changes makes the adjustment process less frightening and more empowering for individuals.

BOUNCING BACK FROM SETBACKS

Preparation cannot eliminate every setback which naturally occurs. The path of life brings about setbacks which include unproductive days and failed deadlines and abandoned plans. Avoiding failure completely is not the goal since learning recovery methods and continuing forward remains the essential objective.

What It Means to Bounce Back

The ability to move forward when facing obstacles is what defines resilience. Resilience serves as the motivating power which drives athletes to train harder following losses and students to persist through poor exam results while professionals use it to rise after facing setbacks. People can develop resilience through purposeful training because the skill exists beyond natural birthright.

Strategies to Bounce Back from Setbacks

- **Reframe Setbacks as Learning Opportunities:** A setback should not be considered a failure because it presents valuable learning possibilities. You should ask yourself what valuable lessons you can extract from this experience. Every piece of failure brings useful information which you can use to direct your future steps.

- **Avoid Dwelling on Negativity:** Single negative experiences cannot determine the path of your life. You should avoid dwelling on past mistakes by dedicating your energy toward developing different strategies for future attempts. Changing your attention to potential solutions will help keep you moving forward.

- **Practice Self-Compassion:** Give yourself the same compassionate understanding that you would give to a friend during such a situation. Remember that every person must face obstacles while the value of your existence remains unaffected by one minor setback.

- **Develop a Backup Plan:** To ensure success you should develop backup plans because unexpected events may occur. Backup plans beyond B can decrease anxiety levels and provide better methods for handling difficulties.

- **Celebrate Small Victories:** Small accomplishments demonstrate the advancement you have achieved. Recognizing small achievements helps you develop self-assurance and proves to yourself that you can handle bigger problems that come your way.

Ava carefully examined her failures at school instead of feeling defeated by test results or social situations. She used this analysis to change her methods. She used each failure to build resilience which eventually gave her strength to tackle upcoming difficulties.

The third step focuses on developing flexibility as well as problem-solving abilities.

Being flexible means adjusting to new circumstances while generating innovative solutions for problems that emerge from failed initial plans. Finding new ways to adjust your path when life delivers unexpected challenges leads to great value in such situations.

CULTIVATING FLEXIBILITY

"You should inquire about the most beneficial next course of action."

To overcome obstacles, you should divide the challenge into more workable components. The present action you need to perform should be your focus instead of letting the whole issue consume you.

- **Be Open to Multiple Approaches:** The solution to any challenge does not require a single perfect method. A failed plan A should prompt you to implement either plan B or C or to combine multiple approaches for a solution. The act of being open will help you discover fresh avenues and resolutions.

- **Embrace the Silver Lining:** Every difficult change brings about an unknown advantage. Moving to a different city initially produces a depressing sensation yet allows you to access innovative growth possibilities.

- **Engage in Creative Problem-Solving:** Set a routine to tackle puzzles and brainstorm together with creative projects. The activities help you develop innovative thinking skills which you can apply to handle actual life challenges.

- **Stay Curious:** Develop an attitude which makes you actively explore everything surrounding you. New situations should be met with an open mind to discover knowledge. Curiosity enables people to convert feelings of anxiety into feelings of excitement while discovering new solutions to problems.

Ava demonstrates flexible behavior when she starts attending a different school. She managed her transition to a new school through focusing on small steps first by joining clubs and local events and reaching out to new classmates which added up to her overall adaptation process. The willingness to try new things allowed her to reduce fear and discover fresh chances as well as new social connections.

THE POWER OF SELF-COMPASSION ALONG WITH POSITIVE THINKING

The way you look at change depends entirely on your frame of mind. Self-compassion together with positive thinking function as effective methods to handle difficult situations instead of allowing a negative mindset to blow things out of proportion.

Strategies for Cultivating a Positive Mindset

- **Practice Positive Affirmations:** Replace negative thoughts with supportive, uplifting statements. Instead of saying, "I can't handle this," try saying, "These challenges help me grow and learn new things." Repeating these affirmations will gradually shift your mindset and strengthen your ability to handle tough situations.

- **Maintain a Gratitude Journal:** Start your day by writing down three factors that bring you gratitude and honor. Small achievements help create positive thinking which allows you to see how much you have advanced. When you speak to yourself in the same way you would comfort a friend then you will find success.

- **Comfort yourself:** When comforting another person through their situation, think about what you would tell them and use that approach to comfort yourself. The development of self-compassion enables you to defeat both self-doubt and the internal criticism you direct at yourself.

- **Set Realistic Expectations:** The process of adapting to change requires a period of time for its completion. Progress at any speed and remember, temporary setbacks are acceptable. Realistic goal-setting helps you lower the stress levels and creates conditions for stable development.

- **Visualize Success:** Devote a few minutes during each day to imagine yourself solving your difficulties with success. Mental preparation through visualization builds your confidence levels as well as helps you face actual challenges.

Through her journey Ava demonstrates how self-compassion works as a powerful force. She developed a habit of replacing negative self-judgments about failure with encouraging thoughts that acknowledged normal struggles and her best efforts. Her changed self-dialogue both reduced her anxiety levels and provided her with new inner strength to handle her current situation optimistically.

Integrating Resilience into Daily Life

Building resilience requires time because it develops through regular practice and dedication toward personal development. Your daily decisions about habits help you build a strong foundation that will carry you through the problems that surely test your strength.

Daily Resilience Practices

- **Morning Reflection:** You should establish a positive intention at the beginning of each morning. Review your abilities because you possess enough strength to handle change and succeed.

- **Mindfulness Exercises:** Practices of mindfulness such as meditation or yoga as well as deep breathing techniques should become part of your daily schedule. These mindfulness techniques lower stress and maintain your concentration ability and create higher wellbeing.

- **Regular Physical Activity:** Exercise is a proven stress-reliever. The combination of walking, jogging or dancing as physical exercise improves your mood and builds your ability to adapt to situations.

- **End-of-Day Journaling:** Wrapping up each day with noting three important things: what worked successfully and what problems occurred alongside what you discovered. Keeping a daily journal enables you to strengthen the wisdom gained from life events while preparing you for upcoming obstacles.

- **Building a Support Network:** Resilience development occurs exclusively through collaborations between individuals. The difference between success and failure emerges when you have supportive people by your side including friends and family and mentors. Presenting the information about your life experiences delivers essential perspective as well as stimulates growth among everyone involved.

- **Peer Support:** Join friends as well as classmates who face comparable challenges in their learning journey. The knowledge that others face similar situations often brings a great sense of comfort to people.

- **Professional Guidance:** When you feel too overwhelmed for managing things on your own then you should consult with either a counselor or therapist. A qualified professional will provide diverse approaches for building your resilience ability.

- **Community Involvement:** Join groups and activities that create feelings of belonging. Your ability to adapt becomes stronger by joining clubs or participating in volunteer activities or local events since these connections form a strong network of support.

Change should be accepted as an opportunity for growth.

Change presents itself through every situation regardless of its magnitude because it brings opportunities for growth. Perceiving obstacles as development chances instead of hopeless hurdles enables the development of resilient strength.

Reframing Your Perspective on Change

- **Reframe the Narrative:** Transform your perspective about change by treating it as a fresh beginning that allows personal reinvention and knowledge acquisition while broadening your world.

- **Set New Goals:** Establish new goals after change so that they fit your current situation. Each purpose functions as a standalone objective that directs you toward diverse prospects in the future.

- **Celebrate Your Adaptability:** Every time you adapt successfully you should give yourself praise regardless of how insignificant the change seems to others. Successes construct your strength for managing obstacles which creates an enduring basis for continued achievement.

Ava demonstrates through her school transition how scary beginnings eventually lead the way to personal development. She learned that every hurdle in her new life became an opportunity to acquire fresh knowledge through her gradual integration into her school activities and establishing new connections. Her small progressions created both psychological strength and personal confidence which turned her fear into a powerful sense of empowerment.

Growth emerges from the process of change

Life presents itself through unexpected changes combined with unexpected obstacles that form its tapestry. Ava demonstrates through her experience that facing life changes leads to personal transformation as well as valuable discoveries about oneself. The combination of accepting change with bouncing back from difficulties, maintaining flexibility and using self-compassion allows you to steer through intense life situations.

Key Takeaways

- **Accept Change:** The natural course of life brings inevitable change which people should accept. It is better to welcome changes than fight them because you will always have something within your control.

- **Bounce Back from Setbacks:** Every failure presents a chance to learn from it. Examine the issues that caused the failure then readjust your strategy before continuing with stronger dedication.

Your commitment to embrace change through life integration of resilience will turn every challenge into an opportunity to create a more promising future. Through its various plot developments, the story of Ava demonstrates that human beings possess remarkable abilities to transition through difficulties while overcoming challenges to thrive.

The next chapter will introduce you to strategies for gaining independence and advocating for yourself as you face future uncertainties and uncover new possibilities. This upcoming challenge will shift the way you see yourself, so stay ready—the adventure is just getting started.

CHAPTER 10

CULTIVATING INDEPENDENCE AND SELF-ADVOCACY

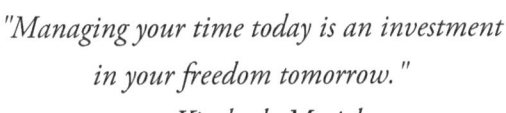

*"Managing your time today is an investment
in your freedom tomorrow."*
— *Kimberly Myrick*

Those surrounding Liam controlled every aspect of his daily life before. Liam followed a regular pattern in which his parents and teachers both alerted him about his schoolwork and directed him through difficult situations. Someone provided guidance regardless of what assignment he forgot or what difficult school subject he encountered. At the beginning of high school, the student experienced a complete transition in his surroundings. As academic requirements increased together with elevated expectations, he became the sole person in charge of managing his time and responsibilities as well as his educational outcomes.

When the responsibility fell on him unexpectedly Liam experienced an initial state of being overwhelmed. The two main questions that plagued him were "How do I handle school work with extracurricular activities and social life?" and "What if I choose poorly?". He gained a sudden comprehension that his achievement would rely on his active control over his personal life. His new understanding starts his progression toward being independent and championing his own needs.

Many people share your feelings about handling personal responsibilities along with your reluctance to express needs. Anyone can sharpen the skills of independence and self-advocacy through practice along with careful thought about experiences.

Why Independence and Self-Advocacy Matter

The ability to be independent does not mean functioning without help yet it requires learning which tasks to lead independently and which ones to request assistance with. Self-advocacy functions together with independence because it enables you to express your demands and establish limits that match your core values. Achieving these capabilities becomes possible through the development of these skills.

→ Schedule maintainers including planners alongside digital calendars and applications help track duties and planning commitments as well as goals.

→ You should analyze possible choices through an assessment that balances their positive aspects against the negative ones to find the most suitable direction.

→ When you require assistance you should approach teachers, mentors or peers to specify the type of help you need.

→ The process of building self-confidence advances through every choice you make regardless of successful outcomes because they both lead to personal advancement.

The adoption of these attributes converts obstacles into learning possibilities that strengthen personal development.

TAKING CHARGE OF YOUR OWN SUCCESS

The cornerstone of independence exists when you grasp that you are in control all aspects of your personal accomplishments. Every mistake provides a chance for personal development and you should stop blaming outside influences for your failures.

How to Embrace Responsibility

→ Build an individual management system for tracking tasks through planners and applications along with basic sticky notes.

→ When you make a mistake, take responsibility and look closely at what went wrong. Then, figure out steps to improve next time.

→ Personal success goals form when you establish specific attainable objectives which express your life dreams.

→ Use your core values to help you make decisions that move you closer to your long-term goals.

Your willingness to take ownership enables you to reconstruct obstacles into paths that lead to improved self-control.

HOW TO MAKE INFORMED DECISIONS AND SOLVE PROBLEMS

Decision-making stands as the fundamental element for achieving independence. A structured method helps reduce the anxiety caused by uncertainty about wrong choices.

Decision-Making Process

→ Create a list of all available choices including joining extracurricular activities and selecting study groups.

→ Establish a balance between assessing positive factors along with possible negative aspects of your choices. This decision will contribute to your personal development because it supports your growth. What challenges might arise?

→ Your confident choice requires flexibility since changes may be necessary. The nature of decisions means that you can adapt your approach whenever conditions in your situation transform.

Use the skills evaluation process to select between joining the debate team or soccer team or taking an after-school job by comparing their benefits against your personal goals. Establishing this process enables people to make independent decisions through informed judgment.

SPEAKING UP AND ADVOCATING FOR YOURSELF

The fear of rejection or judgment causes numerous people to avoid sharing their needs. The practice of self-advocacy enables people to discover fresh possibilities and enhance their access to help.

Strategies for Confident Self-Advocacy

→ You should explain your learning problems by stating "I need help with algebra" so you can review problems with someone. Clear communication minimizes misunderstandings.

→ Select a period of quietness to approach someone because it enables them to provide complete attention.

→ Confident body language requires you to look directly at others and keep your posture straight followed by clear vocal delivery. Your non-verbal communication supports the information you present.

→ Use a respectful tone to state your needs firmly. Your confident approach attracts both respect and more successful support from others.

Role-play practice with a teacher or mentor will help you develop essential skills which you need for expressing needs in genuine circumstances.

OVERCOMING INDEPENDENCE CHALLENGES

A straight path to independence occurs seldom in life. Every challenge which arises to test your determination offers you valuable learning experiences.

Common Challenges and How to Overcome Them

→ Normal mistakes are essential for personal growth so fear should not stop you from progressing. Study every mistake to extract valuable lessons from it.

→ To cope with overwhelming situations, you can divide your tasks into multiple smaller steps that you can handle step-by-step. Working on one task element at a time helps avoid burnout symptoms.

→ Establish meaningful goals that you can easily remember and keep their importance in mind. The establishment of personal rewards helps people stay motivated.

→ Begin by asking for small low-risk assistance so you can develop your ability to request help. With practice you will develop the ability to address bigger problems that appear in the future.

Every challenge you conquer enables you to master upcoming obstacles therefore showing that becoming independent means continuous personal development.

Taking Charge of Your Own Success

Developing independence and self-advocacy practice transforms the way you deal with life. Successful achievement of a meaningful future comes through your commitment to accountable conduct while you decide wisely and express yourself with self-assurance.

Remember:

→ Taking responsibility means both embracing your actions along with gaining knowledge from every encounter you encounter.

→ You should utilize a systematic process to determine wise choices.

→ Express your needs to others while seeking help when you need it.

→ You should welcome every challenge because it lets you build up your resilience besides growing your confidence levels.

The journey doesn't end here. Your next development task involves creating healthy routines which will lead to long-term success. Chapter 11 explains strategies to develop lasting habits which link your objectives to personal wellness enhancement.

Do you want to control your behaviors and create a life for your dreams? Moving ahead will help you discover your complete potential.

CHAPTER 11

BUILDING HEALTHY
HABITS AND ROUTINES

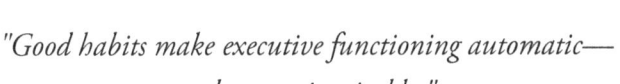

*"Good habits make executive functioning automatic—
and success inevitable."*
—Kimberly Myrick

N oah's story reveals how he remains stuck in a cycle of unhelpful habits.

Each morning, he recognizes that better time management would bring greater success, yet he continually struggles with procrastination and misses new opportunities. He vows to wake up early to exercise before school and in the afternoon to finish his homework, then reward himself with video games. Instead, he repeatedly presses the snooze button, convincing himself he needs just five more minutes of rest. A quick glance at his phone then turns into extended scrolling, consuming half an hour until he's forced to leave at the last minute. By the time Noah returns home, he's exhausted and sets aside his study plans to rest—followed by yet more screen time.

Noah didn't seem lazy; rather, he simply lacked effective strategies to break his negative behavioral patterns. His experience reflects what many people face when trying to establish healthy routines but remain stuck, unable to take action. Habits are often misunderstood, as they arise from a combination of careful planning and consistent daily effort.

The following discussion will focus on habit research together with successful routine development approaches as well as solutions for turning destructive habits into productive patterns. By using appropriate methods, you can develop a daily schedule which provides immediate success benefits while evolving your life in the long term.

WHY HABITS AND ROUTINES MATTER

Your morning, afternoon and evening routines are primarily determined by your habits when you perform tasks like tooth brushing and mobile device checking. The brain chooses routines because such patterns reduce energy usage through task automation. Good habits create an efficient operation of daily life by lowering stress while offering dependable structure which allows your brain to concentrate on advanced choices.

Benefits of Healthy Habits

- **Enhanced Productivity:** Your daily routines limit the decision fatigue that helps you concentrate on the essential matters in life. The adoption of healthy habits allows you to perform better through decreased mental analysis of your activities.

- **Stress Reduction:** Your scheduled routines eliminate everyday uncertainties which reduces both stress and nervousness in your life. The knowledge of upcoming events lets your mind achieve relaxation so it can focus on present tasks.

- **Improved Focus and Discipline:** The practice of maintaining routine practices allows your brain to develop the ability to maintain focus. Your automatic behavior proficiency together with resilience levels increase through repetition.

- **Accelerated Achievement:** Regular minor activities develop into major long-term achievements. Definite progress toward your goals occurs through all your chosen beneficial actions which continue to increase in power.

Bad habits demonstrate the same level of strength as good habits when they function to destroy your most important goals. Your task now becomes to retrain your brain for replacing negative habits with positive ones.

Understanding How Habits Work

Every habit contains three essential elements which form the Habit Loop structure consisting of Cue followed by Routine then Reward. Knowledge about the Habit Loop provides all essential information needed to transform your habits.

The Habit Loop

- **Cue:** The beginning of any habit-triggering event. When Noah starts his day he typically notices two key triggers including feeling sleepy upon waking or experiencing uninteresting moments in the morning.

- **Routine:** The behavior itself. The daily pattern for Noah starts by pressing snooze and moving to his phone screen.

- **Reward:** The positive outcome which your brain acquires from performing a particular action. The fast entertainment experience followed by quick relaxation brings immediate reward to Noah when he wakes up feeling tired or feels bored.

Your brain learns to connect the cue with a reward through time which transforms the routine into an automatic response. You must interrupt this cycle to eliminate a bad habit.

Changing the Habit Loop

- **Identify the Cue:** Start by pinpointing the events which cause your unwanted behavior to occur. Think about the emotions which come right before you press the snooze button. Being awake early or wishing to sleep longer appears to be the factors triggering the behavior.

- **Replace the Routine:** You should replace your negative routine when you determine the cue trigger. The first step to break this habit is to rise from bed immediately without phone contact and perform either a brief stretching routine or mindfulness practice.

- **Alter the Reward:** Alter the Reward: Your brain needs a new, positive stimulus to replace the current behavior pattern. Rather than spending time scrolling through social media, switch to more beneficial activities—such as taking a refreshing shower and preparing a nutritious breakfast—so you can start your day on a productive note.

Through deliberate intervention of the Habit Loop your brain will learn to create better health-oriented routines. Repeated practice of new routines leads to their growth in strength until they replace outdated habits completely.

Developing healthy habits takes time and appropriate planning together with continuous effort and suitable methods.

How to Build Strong, Lasting Habits

- **Start Small:** You should begin with an achievable objective rather than establishing an ambitious target like daily hour-long exercise because starting with five minutes of morning stretching is more achievable. People who accomplish small tasks discover personal success which motivates them to attempt larger goals.

- **Habit Stacking:** Every new habit should link directly with an already established daily practice. A quick stretching period should be directly followed by your morning tooth brushing routine. A useful technique enables us to link habits for natural integration in our day.

- **Make It Easy:** Create an environment without obstacles that blocks your new habit from forming. Prepare your workout clothes before bedtime and place your reading material near your bed for night reading and disable phone notifications when you study.

- **Use a Habit Tracker:** Following your advancement objectives becomes substantially motivating. The visual representation of your progress through physical checklists or Habitica app allows you to strengthen your dedication towards new habits.

- **Celebrate Milestones:** Provide yourself with recognition for every advancement that you achieve throughout your journey. Getting rewards for your goals achievement helps you stay motivated while strengthening positive actions through small treats and additional leisure time.

Examples of Habit Stacking

- **Morning Routine:** Begin your day by waking up at 7 AM and drinking a glass of water before stretching for five minutes followed by a nutritious breakfast. The carefully arranged morning activities establish a positive atmosphere during the whole day.

- **After-School Routine:** Home arrival should be followed by a short period of relaxation before spending 10 minutes reviewing notes followed by homework completion through focused time blocks.

- **Night Routine:** To prepare for bed you need to turn off all screens thirty minutes early and read from a book or journal before going to sleep at a scheduled time. Sleep quality enhances through this routine and it establishes conditions for successful future workdays.

These strategies help you develop step-by-step a structure which leads to long-term achievement. Consistency plays the main role because each positive action you make builds upon itself to establish permanent changes.

OVERCOMING BAD HABITS AND REPLACING THEM

The process of overcoming bad habits requires substituting existing behaviors with new ones rather than confronting the habit head-on.

How to Replace Bad Habits

- **Make the Bad Habit Harder to Perform:** You should place your phone in another space when you want to avoid first-morning phone checks. When temptation is eliminated, it becomes simpler to establish new routines.

- **Make the Good Habit Easier:** The placement of a book on your nightstand improves your chances of reading before sleeping. When new habits become simpler to perform then people will maintain them.

- **Leverage Accountability:** Tell someone about your goals because they will help you maintain your focus toward your goals. This type of consistent monitoring both motivates and gives support.

- **Celebrate Every Success:** Each time you create a healthy habit from an unwanted behavior you should treat yourself. Your progress recognition builds dedication and enhances the attractiveness of your new habit.

Example: Replacing a Late-Night Screen Habit

- **Old Habit:** The habit of watching TikTok followed by social media scrolling occurs before bedtime.

- **New Habit:** You should dedicate ten minutes to reading or spend time journaling about what happened during your day.

- **Strategy:** Place your phone in a different area while you charge it and maintain reading or journaling materials near your bed. When you maintain your new daily routine throughout the day you should give yourself a small reward as a nightly celebration.

The exchange of harmful behaviors with beneficial ones enhances your regular schedule and creates space in your mind for additional productive work. Positive routines build upon each other to create extensive improvements between productivity and wellness levels.

CREATING A SUSTAINABLE DAILY ROUTINE

A productive life depends on having an organized daily routine system. Routines work as automatic systems that decrease the necessity for ongoing decisions thus enabling you to concentrate on essential matters.

Building an Effective Daily Routine

A standard routine consists of distinct periods for morning activities combined with afternoon and evening sections. Here's how to create one:

Morning Routine

The schedule you follow during morning time determines how your entire day will unfold. A morning routine that is strong creates success-ready conditions for your mind and body.

- **Wake Up at a Consistent Time:** You should pick one specific wake-up time for every day to maintain a healthy body cycle.

- **Hydrate and Stretch:** Start your day with water consumption followed by a few stretching movements to wake up your physical system.

- **Healthy Breakfast:** Eat nutritious food to gain enhanced concentration and increased energy levels for your body.

- **Plan Your Top Three Tasks:** Choose the three activities which demand the highest priority for today. You should concentrate your energy toward essential goals by keeping your focus.

After-School or Work Routine

Devote your post-activity hours to organizing your time between work commitments and relaxation time.

- **Take a Short Break:** Take a brief 15-minute rest period as your transition from relaxation to studying or work activities.

- **Focused Study/Work Blocks:** Create smaller work segments which include specific objectives to reach. The Pomodoro method provides a technique for sustaining your concentration.

- **Physical Activity:** Physical activities both inside and outside will help you refresh your mind and gain more energy.

- **Review Your Progress:** Each work session should end with a brief check of your completed tasks.

Night Routine

You need a regular night routine to prepare for restful sleep because it builds your productivity through better sleep quality.

- **Screen-Free Time Before Bed:** All electronic screens should be turned off thirty minutes before your bedtime because it decreases stimulation levels.

- **Reflect and Journal:** Note down three items that you are grateful for or analyze your daily achievements. The practice strengthens positive mental attitudes.

- **Set a Consistent Bedtime:** Make it a habit to be in bed (without your phone, tablet, laptop or TV) within the same hour daily in order to achieve sleep cycle normalization.

Your daily routine should address every aspect of your day which turns your daily behaviors into automatic habits. The establishment of a scheduled day helps decrease decision fatigue because it enables regular practice of healthy behaviors.

Build the Life You Want

Your current life activities define what will become of your future. All your daily activities regardless of their size determine both your personal growth and the future direction of your life. Having good habits together with established routines builds the basis for success while keeping you productive as well as lowering your stress and building momentum to reach your future objectives.

Key Takeaways

- **Understand the Habit Loop:** Every habit follows a three-step pattern: a cue triggers a routine, which is followed by a reward. By breaking the cycle of bad habits, you can replace them with new, positive behaviors.

- **Develop Positive Habits:** Begin by making your habits small and connecting them to your daily routines then utilize habit trackers as well as other tools for reinforcing your habit development. Consistent performance of new habits leads to their permanent integration as lasting habits.

- **Replace Bad Habits:** The key is to make it harder to engage in unwanted actions while offering healthier alternatives. Rewards and accountability can help make this transition smoother and more effective.

- **Establish a Daily Routine:** Structure your day with dedicated routines for the morning, after-school or work, and nighttime. A properly designed schedule enables you to develop positive habits while boosting your productivity levels.

- **The Power of Consistency:** Building lasting habits takes time and patience, usually anywhere from 21 to 66 days. Your commitment and persistence will pay off, with even small changes leading to meaningful progress.

Establishing healthy routines takes more time than a single dramatic change would. The development into habits moves slower than many people expect yet continues thanks to continuous dedication and personal examination. Each day presents a chance to practice beneficial behaviors while abandoning those habits which no longer benefit you. Every minor advancement you make creates a future that includes high productivity alongside balance and success.

The following consideration will make you contemplate:

The skills you learned for habit formation may test your discipline because you succeed in developing better daily routines. The digital world which has become a fundamental part of our current way of life may begin interfering with the equilibrium you have carefully established.

We will study technological use for executive functioning in the following chapter because this examines methods to benefit from digital systems without falling into digital overload. What are the exact methods through which you can achieve complete digital connectivity without becoming uncontrollable?

As Noah acquires meaningful accomplishments by waking up on time and finishing his homework while adding hobbies to his schedule a fresh obstacle emerges to destroy his recently constructed structure. A sudden digital distraction wave along with endless scrolling temptations rises into view to challenge all his hard work. Holds the answer whether Noah will keep his newfound discipline intact as technology attempts to reclaim its former dominance.

We will continue to the following chapter which focuses on the struggle between digital ease and mindful productivity. Your search for the answer could reshape the way you manage technology and wellness habits in your life. Are you prepared to uncover the secret?

Use of these strategies leads to more than simple habit formation because they establish the essential structure needed for succeeding in life. Your achievements through positive actions build your goal achievement capacity while forming a future where productivity combines with well-being. Your next task requires you to determine how technology will assist your habit development instead of allowing it to control your daily activities.

CHAPTER 12

LEVERAGING TECHNOLOGY FOR EXECUTIVE FUNCTIONING

"Innovation is an outcome of a habit not a random act"
—Sukant Ratnakar

Technology served as her essential tools as Riley enjoyed its presence because she relied on her phone, laptop and tablet as essential parts of her daily life. She relied on these devices for her coursework as well as communication with friends while she monitored social media activities. The resource which initially made her so successful became too heavy for her to carry when time passed. Daily life for Riley became an overwhelming experience because she faced an endless barrage of emails and notifications and multiple reminders. Her digital environment consisted of multiple devices with numerous applications and documents which made locating the starting point seem impossible.

On that homework evening Riley planned to take a brief text message break but before she knew it grew into ten messages and a scroll through social media which used up an entire hour of her study time. She grew frustrated when she understood that technology which was supposed to simplify her daily tasks instead led her toward continuous digital confusion along with constant interruptions.

Many people share Riley's experience because they face continuous interruptions and disarray due to technology usage. Technology functions as both an advantage and a disadvantage in the contemporary world. Everyone should leverage technology as their most powerful asset for success yet failure to control it leads to non stop distractions and excess mental stress.

The following section provides instructions for using technology effectively in organizational tasks and time management and productivity while preventing digital overload.

Why Technology Can Be a Double-Edged Sword

Technology delivers three great benefits to users through its quick knowledge retrieval capabilities and its efficient tools and its instant communication features. However, the advantage technological innovations provide also delivers an overwhelming number of notifications and information as well as multiple avenues for being drawn away from the present moment. People who harness technology as an effective tool must first understand how they will utilize it instead of letting technology dominate their activities.

The endless potential of digital systems threatens to exceed the organizational abilities of any person who does not implement proper management techniques. The initial step for technology utilization in executive functioning requires understanding its strengths together with its potential weaknesses.

DIGITAL TOOLS FOR ORGANIZATION AND PRODUCTIVITY

Technology provides you with its most important benefit which is organization management. Digital tools operate as personal assistants to maintain track of all critical information beyond memory-based storage systems.

Best Tools for Staying Organized

- **Note-Taking Apps:** Three note-taking applications including Evernote, OneNote and Google Keep provide users with the ability to write down thoughts and important notes and reminders. You maintain organization by storing all your notes at one central location which prevents the mess created by random sticky notes along with lost memos.

- **Digital Calendars:** Users benefit from Google Calendar and Apple Calendar software because these programs let them organize days by scheduling tasks while setting reminder alerts. Your day operates efficiently while avoiding deadline slips since calendar alerts happen automatically.

- **Cloud Storage:** Google Drive together with Dropbox and OneDrive enable users to store their files securely through accessible platforms. Every document along with your photos and projects remain structured and easily accessible across all your locations.

- **Task Management Apps:** Managed projects through the use of apps including Todoist, Microsoft To-Do and Trello provide users with task breakdown capabilities. The apps enable users to build to-do lists and monitor their development while recognizing minor achievements.

How to Use These Tools Effectively

- **Centralize Your Information:** A single application should contain all your notes and reminders to avoid information loss between different platforms.

- **Set Calendar Alerts:** Set up alerts together with notifications to remember important deadlines as well as significant events.

- **Organize Files into Folders:** Your cloud storage needs a clear folder organization which allows you to find your documents quickly.

- **Maintain a Daily To-Do List:** The daily update of your task management app includes checking off tasks that you have finished. The pictorial display functions as a motivational tool that tracks your progress successfully.

Using digital organizational tools throughout your regular schedule allows you to create stronger productivity and better organization which simplifies the management of jam-packed schedules.

TIME MANAGEMENT APPLICATIONS & SCHEDULING HACKS

The modern world which depends on constant connectivity makes effective time management more difficult than before. Digital interruptions lead people to accidentally waste their time. Specific time management apps together with scheduled methods aid users in bringing their days back under their control.

Best Time Management Apps

- **Focus Booster & Pomodone:** Time management applications make it possible to put the Pomodoro Technique into practice through its system of working in focused segments (typically 25 minutes) interspersed with short recovery periods. The approach helps both users focus better and work more efficiently.

- **RescueTime & Screen Time:** Screen Time and RescueTime enable users to measure app and website usage duration thus helping them detect disturbances which then guides them toward better behavioral changes.

- **Google Calendar & Notion:** These tools enable users to select particular times for both work and rest intervals which helps to develop effective time distribution throughout each day.

How to Manage Your Time with Technology

- **Use Time-Blocking:** Each day should contain organized periods of time for working, studying, taking breaks and resting. The system enables you to distribute proper focus among all your daily responsibilities.

- **Track Screen Time:** Track your time on distracting applications by using monitoring apps to establish usage limits. Establish boundaries to minimize your time wastage.

- **Schedule Focus Sessions:** The Pomodoro Technique helps you structure your daily tasks. The schedule includes working intensely for 25 minutes followed by scheduled rest periods of 5 minutes then repeating the sequence.

- **Activate "Do Not Disturb" Mode:** Your work performance will be uninterrupted by notifications which could disrupt your concentration. The implementation of this strategy allows you to maintain focus while reducing the number of interruptions.

You can plan your day using the given time management tools to boost productivity while controlling digital interferences.

MINDFULNESS AND STRESS MANAGEMENT APPS

The same technology that causes mental distraction can serve as an instrument to enhance clarity while decreasing daily stress levels. Relaxation and mindfulness applications provide you with meditative guides together with soothing sounds which assist you in finding mental clarity while lowering stress.

Best Apps for Mindfulness & Relaxation

- **Headspace & Calm:** Software applications offer steered mediation techniques which assists users in controlling their stress while enhancing their focus until they begin the new day with mental clarity.

- **Forest App:** Through its innovative design the app prompts users to focus on device-free activities by letting them grow virtual trees. Spending more time without using your device results in growing your virtual tree larger.

- **Noisli & Brain.fm:** These apps provide specially created sounds and music which enhance concentration abilities and develop a peaceful environment free from distractions.

How to Use These Apps Effectively

- **Start Your Day with Meditation:** Start your day by meditating for a short period to create a positive mood for the upcoming hours.

- **Utilize Focus Music or White Noise:** Background sounds which block distractions and maintain focus should be used during study or work periods.

- **Schedule Regular Digital Breaks:** The mindfulness apps will help you schedule brief screen-free periods which let your mind find relaxation.

Mindfulness techniques enable people to transform technology from a stress source into an instrument that helps them gain mental clarity along with better focus abilities.

BALANCING SCREEN TIME AND AVOIDING DIGITAL OVERLOAD

Digital overload exists as a genuine menace against productivity together with well-being. Large amounts of screen interaction create harm to sleep patterns and diminishes the power to focus as well as elevating stress levels. The essential practice requires employing technology to boost productivity without losing sight of essential unconnected time.

Strategies to Control Screen Time

- **Set App Limits:** Your devices include built-in features that enable you to establish daily limits on applications which distract you. The feature stops you from devoting extended periods to social media or other activities.

- **Create Phone-Free Zones:** Devote specific periods and designated home locations to phone-free zones which include both study areas and dining spaces.

- **Establish a Digital Wind-Down Routine:** You should deactivate your screen for at least thirty minutes before you go to sleep. Screens with blue light disrupt your sleep patterns by causing difficulties in resting.

- **Adopt the "One-Tab Rule":** Browsing the internet should involve working with only one browser tab at a time because it helps you stay focused and reduces distractions.

Taking control of your screen usage allows you to use technology as a helpful device without letting it become a continuous disruption.

Utilize Technology As Your Ally Instead of Becoming Its Slave.

Correct utilization of technology enables it to serve as your most powerful asset in reaching success. Digital tools that help you organize and manage time and practice mindfulness and productivity enable you to establish a balanced routine with enhanced efficiency and reduced stress.

Recap of Key Strategies

- **Organization:** Your information should be central through note-taking applications and digital calendars and cloud storage together with task management platforms.

- **Time Management:** Implement time-blocking and screen time tracking along with focus sessions as organizational methods to build daily structures that reduce disruptive elements.

- **Mindfulness:** To manage stress along with anxiety and improve mental awareness you should use mindfulness apps in combination with stress management apps.

- **Screen Time Control:** Establish boundaries that ensure specific areas without technology will protect you from continuously looking at screens and receiving notifications.

You can build an operational digital space which optimizes your objectives while driving productivity by learning these control techniques. Instead of being a chaotic force technology will transform into a tool which assists your organization and concentration. Once you master technology usage for effectiveness a new threat emerges in your path.

Your new found time management skills and organizational methods along with technology tools becomes irrelevant when your motivation disappears. Despite possessing excellent apps and planners along with effective strategies they will not succeed unless you maintain discipline in using them. What strategy should you use to move ahead when you lack motivation? Your plan for staying consistent is active even when your drive disappears during those weak moments. The following section will demonstrate the approach. The secrets to self-discipline and long-term motivation will be exposed in the following chapter to help you maintain your path regardless of the circumstances.

CHAPTER 13

STRENGTHENING SELF-DISCIPLINE AND MOTIVATION

———————— ❖ ————————

*"Strengthening executive functioning skills
transforms potential into reality."*
— Lynn Meltzer

Jack had big plans: he wanted to beat everyone to the punch by waking up early, working out daily, and finishing all his tasks ahead of time. Each Sunday night, he'd map out a perfect schedule, sure that this week would finally be different. Monday kicked off strong—he was up before the alarm, hit the gym, and got school assignments done early. But as the week went on, his motivation started slipping. By Wednesday, he was hitting the snooze button over and over, skipping workouts, and telling himself he'd study later. When the weekend rolled around, all his careful planning went out the window. He ended up scrolling through social media instead of reading, putting his assignments off until the last minute, and making the same old promise to do better next week.

Jack initially pointed to low motivation as the reason behind his erratic behavior. The real nature of motivation varies from self-discipline since self-discipline functions as a learnable skill. His case mirrors those of numerous people who encounter challenges when they aim to maintain consistent goal pursuit. Self-discipline functions like any other muscle because it can undergo training to strengthen itself. After construction it acts as your driving force on days when your motivation levels are low.

In this chapter you will learn how to develop unbreakable self-discipline followed by methods to overcome obstacles and create systems which turn progress into a regular habit, not just sporadic motivational bursts.

Why Motivation Alone Isn't Enough

Motivation produces remarkable inspiration during its presence. A motivational speech can create unstoppable feelings while achieving a fresh objective produces adrenaline spikes. Once the original motivating force fades away the desire to keep going disappears. The following points describe the nature of motivation:

→ Your morning inspiration tends to vanish during the course of the day.

→ The beginning passion for new habits spreads quickly but obstacles in the way make people lose their drive toward progress.

→ You promise yourself to complete the task tomorrow yet discover tomorrow constantly pushes the task into the distant future.

Successful people understand that motivation can be unpredictable, so they build strong systems to create lasting progress. Relying on motivation alone doesn't lead to real results; instead, you need to develop discipline—the ability to stay consistent, even when your mood changes..

Discipline enables you to rise early during frigid mornings while forcing yourself to exercise when rest is more appealing and to study despite numerous distractions. Your commitment stays unbroken because discipline transforms inspirational ideas into productive actions even though motivation levels may change.

THE SCIENCE BEHIND SELF-DISCIPLINE

Using self-discipline serves as a workout for your mental strength because regular practice will improve your abilities. Understanding the brain's processes with regard to instant reward choices against future benefits helps us create strategies to strengthen our discipline abilities

The Two Competing Forces in Your Brain:

- **Instant Gratification (The Limbic System):** The limbic system operates as a brain region that looks for immediate satisfaction. Such choices are the reason why you would decide to use social media, eat junk food and watch countless episodes of your preferred show. Your limbic system delivers immediate rewards which makes short-term pleasures seem exceptionally attractive to you.

- **Long-Term Thinking (The Prefrontal Cortex):** The prefrontal cortex is the part of your brain that helps you plan, make decisions, and control impulses. It lets you think about the long-term benefits of your actions— like how regular exercise can improve your health or how studying consistently can boost your grades.

When you give in to immediate impulses, it strengthens the part of your brain responsible for quick emotional reactions (the limbic system). On the other hand, choosing actions that offer long-term rewards—despite providing less immediate satisfaction—helps strengthen the prefrontal cortex, which improves your ability to make thoughtful, goal-driven decisions.

How to Strengthen Your Self-Discipline Muscle

- **Start Small:** Begin with tiny challenges. Every night tidy your room and workspace or lay out your clothes for the next day. Or every morning, set time to make your bed. The choice is yours. The daily practice teaches you to complete what you start.

- **Practice Delayed Gratification:** Develop a habit of waiting before receiving your rewards. Your homework should always take precedence over YouTube or social media because completing your assignments first allows you to relax afterward as a positive reinforcement.

- **Adopt a "No Choice" Rule:** During exercise or study time refrain from holding inner discussions about it. There are no exceptions during workout time so put on your shoes right now to complete your exercise.

- **Track Your Progress:** A habit tracker along with a journal allows you to document all your daily milestones. Your growing streaks deliver concrete signs of improvement which makes you continue your path forward.

Repeated practice of these tiny disciplinary actions will naturally make them simpler to perform. These small acts build up into a forceful habit which moves you forward regardless of motivational dips.

HOW TO BUILD MENTAL TOUGHNESS AND STAY CONSISTENT

Among the foundations of discipline stands consistent action at all times. You should perform your tasks even when you lack motivation since this proves to be the secret for progress. Procrastination persists endlessly when people delay important tasks for both the perfect moment or when motivation strikes.

Why We Struggle with Motivation

- **Overwhelming Tasks:** When a task feels huge, it can be hard to even start. The fix? Break it down into smaller steps. That way, it feels way more doable and way less overwhelming.

- **Waiting for Motivation:** If you're waiting to *feel* motivated before you start, you might never get going. The truth is, taking action creates motivation—not the other way around. So start small, and the momentum will follow.

- **Temptations and Distractions:** With distractions everywhere, it's important to cut out temptations— they can easily throw you off track and mess with your goals.

The 2-Minute Rule: A Simple Trick to Beat Procrastination

The 2-Minute Rule is an easy but powerful way to help you stop putting things off. The idea is simple: when you're struggling to get started, commit to doing the task for just two minutes. That's it. Here's why it works:

- **It's Easy to Start:** Two minutes feels totally doable, so it's way less overwhelming. That tiny step helps you break through the mental block of getting started.

- **It Builds Momentum:** Once you begin, it's easier to keep going. That small action can kick off a chain reaction and help you stay on a roll.

Next time you're avoiding homework or studying, just tell yourself: "I'll read for two minutes." Most of the time, those two minutes turn into ten, twenty, or even more. The hardest part is starting—and this trick makes that part easier.

Creating a Consistency System That Works for You

- **Set Daily Non-Negotiables:** Pick one activity that you will commit to doing every single day, no matter what. For example, reading for 10 minutes in the morning can become a non-negotiable part of your routine. The key is to choose something small and manageable, so it's easy to stick with every day.

- **Use the 5-Second Rule:** When you feel yourself procrastinating, countdown from 5 to 1, and then immediately start the task. This quick countdown disrupts the urge to delay and forces your brain into action before it can talk you out of it.

- **Make Tasks Fun:** Turn tasks you find boring into something enjoyable. Want to study? Listen to your favorite music or turn it into a game by setting a time challenge. The more fun you can make it, the easier it is to stick with it.

- **Build a Supportive Environment:** Surround yourself with people who are focused and disciplined. Having friends who are also committed to their goals can push you to stay on track. Discipline is contagious, and the more you surround yourself with motivated people, the easier it is to stay consistent.

- **Create a System That Works Beyond Motivation:** Your system should be designed to work even when motivation is low. By creating a routine of non-negotiables, fun tasks, and positive influences, you're building a consistent plan that doesn't rely on how you're feeling on any given day. With time, these habits will become automatic and much easier to maintain.

Feeling stuck or unmotivated isn't a permanent state—it just means you haven't found the right strategies yet. Often, it's not about a lack of effort, but a lack of structure or a clear plan.

When you create a system that fits your style and goals, taking action becomes easier and progress starts to flow.

These strategies help break the habit of procrastination. By taking small, consistent actions, you build the foundation for self-discipline and train yourself to take action more easily.

CREATING A PERSONAL MOTIVATION PLAN

Even the most disciplined version of you will have off days—it's totally normal. That's why having a personal motivation plan is so helpful. It's like a backup plan that keeps you on track when your energy or drive starts to dip.

Elements of an Effective Motivation Plan

- **Find Your "Why":** Think about why your goals matter to you. Is it to land your dream job one day, feel more confident, or just build a life you're proud of? Write it down. When you're feeling unmotivated or ready to give up, go back to that "why" to remind yourself what you're working for.

- **Set Clear, Tangible Rewards:** Find out what will motivate you to do the tasks. For example, if you have come to the end of a challenging project then go ahead and reward yourself by doing something you love.

- **Visualize Success:** Visualise the outcomes that you desire each day. Imagine how good it would feel to reach the desired goals. Not just that visualization also keeps your motivation up and it reinforces your commitment.

- **Surround Yourself with the Right People:** Interact with people who are motivated and disciplined. Often, they will be able to provide you with enough energy and encouragement to keep you going in the right direction of your own goals.

- **Establish Accountability:** Tell someone you trust your goals and ask him or her to hold you accountable. Gentle reminders to keep you on track are regular check-ins.

- **Create a Written Plan:** Along with documenting daily, weekly and monthly goals and what you will do to achieve them. Keep reviewing this plan so that you can monitor your progress and make necessary changes.

Alex discovered that developing a personal motivation plan changed his approach to how he did daily tasks. No matter how much or how little motivation he had, there was a plan that kept him moving forward. As these strategies grew in his life, over time his ability to stay consistent got better and his productivity increased.

The Discipline is the Key to Success

Self-discipline is the cornerstone of the journey to achieving your goals. The initial fire is sparked by motivation, but it is discipline that will keep the fire burning long after the initial excitement has died down.

Recap of Key Strategies

- **Strengthen Your Discipline Muscle:** Take small steps forward first with small presentable tasks and progressively improve to bigger ones. Each act of discipline makes you more and more able to succeed.

- **Take Action When Motivation Fades:** The 2 minute and 5 second rules can be used to start your activities and keep moving forward even when you are unmotivated.

- **Break Down Overwhelming Tasks:** When a task feels too big, it's easy to avoid it. The solution? Break it into smaller, manageable steps. Suddenly, what felt impossible becomes doable.

- **Create a Personal Motivation Plan:** Determine your 'why', set rewards, see yourself succeed, and get support from supportive people. This is a safety net for days when your natural motivation may fail.

- **Consistent, Daily Practice:** Self-discipline isn't built overnight—it's developed through consistent effort over time. Every small step you take trains your brain to take action, even when you don't feel like it.

They give you a powerful system; by mastering these strategies you are given a method to stay consistent but more importantly, how you change your approach to problems. With self-discipline becoming your reliable partner in the journey to success, you will be ready to tackle setbacks, deal with procrastination and build a life of success.

While Alex slowly started seeing real progress—waking up early, sticking to his workouts, and turning in assignments on time—he began to believe that self-discipline was the secret sauce to success. This steady routine made him more confident, and for the first time, his goals felt totally within reach. Everything was finally falling into place for Alex—until an unexpected curveball changed everything: a massive project with a tight deadline landed in his lap. It required skills he hadn't mastered and teamwork he wasn't used to. Worst of all, it came loaded with surprises that threatened to unravel the systems he'd worked so hard to build.

With pressure mounting and no clear solution in sight, Alex found himself at a crossroads. Could he stick to his habits and stay disciplined in the face of chaos? Or would this challenge reveal the cracks in his carefully built routine? One thing was certain: his self-discipline was about to face its toughest test yet.

Every decision you make, every habit you strengthen, pushes your life in the direction you choose. Looking back on Alex's journey, and imagining the next challenge ahead, consider this:

when life throws something unexpected your way, will you crumble—or will you rise?

The answer lies in your ability to adapt, persevere, and turn every setback into a step forward. Growth doesn't come from staying comfortable. It comes from how you respond when things get tough.

CHAPTER 14

LIFELONG LEARNING AND CONTINUOUS IMPROVEMENT

"Teaching executive functioning skills is teaching students how to learn and how to manage themselves effectively."
— Peg Dawson

Emily was always a dedicated student. Throughout her school years, Emily did everything right—she got good grades, followed the rules, and thrived in a structured routine. But once she made the leap from high school to college, everything changed. There were no more teachers or parents reminding her to study, helping her set goals, or pushing her to aim higher. Suddenly, she was in charge of it all. That's when Emily realized something important: learning doesn't stop after graduation—it's just getting started.

In college she could not keep up her classes. She was falling behind without external reminders. When Emily woke up one morning she scrolled through social media and saw pictures from old classmates, one had already begun a business, one was learning new skills away from the classroom and another had a dream internship. Emily couldn't shake the heavy feeling that she was going nowhere. She thought school was the only place to learn, but now she knew that it is never the end of learning and those who keep on developing never stop learning.

This was a turning point for Emily. She started to realize that success is not only about natural intelligence, but also the capacity to continue learning, changing, evolving. This chapter will help you discover how to stay one step ahead, turn continuous improvement into a habit, and keep learning throughout your life.

Why Lifelong Learning Matters

It is a myth that learning happens only in school. In fact, the most successful people know that learning is a never-ending thing. Several reasons are why lifelong learning is important:

- **The World Is Always Changing:** There are new technologies, new industries and new trends every day. Otherwise, you will find yourself falling behind, out of relevance and ultimately out of competition.

- **Your Brain Stays Sharp:** But engaging in constant learning, not just learning, but improving your hands-on experience by bringing in new skills, improves your memory and problem solving. A healthy mind is a stimulated mind.

- **Opportunities Multiply:** The more you know, the richer the toolkit you have in hand. New skills open doors to exciting careers, innovative projects and personal growth opportunities.

- **Staying Ahead of the Competition:** In the world today, the best jobs and opportunities are given to people who are continuously looking to better themselves. Life dependent learning means that you will never find yourself behind.

The courageous act of continuous learning, while also giving you the ability to do whatever it takes anytime, any day regardless of what challenges come your way.

THE POWER OF NEVER-ENDING LEARNING

The people who stop learning after school believe that formal education means the end of their intellectual journey. Despite that, the most successful people realize that the quest for knowledge never ends.

Embracing Continuous Learning

Bill Gates and Elon Musk, the two are avid readers and world's leader in fields they learned from a certain training. Continuous learning is the foundation to their success; they are able to innovate and beat their industries because of it.

How to Develop a Learning Mindset

- **Stay Curious:** Make it a habit to ask questions. Dig deeper the second you meet something new. Always ask 'Why?' and 'How?' until you have a total comprehension of what you are doing.

- **Read Every Day:** There are sources of new knowledge such as books, articles, podcasts and online courses. A little bit of reading each day will add up over time.

- **Learn from Others:** Surround yourself with a crowd that challenges you and inspires you. Talk to people, attend seminars and find mentors, who ask you to think differently.

- **Be Open to Feedback:** Criticism is not a failure sign; it's a means of improvement. Take feedback you get and learn from that your approach needs to change.

Continuous learning allows your perspective to grow and evolve. The moment you stop seeking new knowledge, you risk getting stuck. But when you commit to learning for life, you unlock the potential to grow without limits.

HOW TO STAY CURIOUS AND KEEP EXPANDING YOUR SKILLS

Fuel for lifelong learning is curiosity. It's the spark that lights the fire within to want to explore new unique ideas, embark on new great experiences and to learn new individual skills.

How to Stay Curious

- **Ask "Why?" and "How?" Frequently:** Never believe all that is said. Go beyond in-depth subjects that interest you and force yourself to understand underlying principles.

- **Try New Experiences:** Go learn a new hobby, visit new places, try to take challenges that are out of your comfort zone. Every new experience is another enrichment for the point of view.

- **Experiment and Explore:** Hands-on experiences— whether through work, personal projects, or trial and error—are some of the most valuable lessons you'll ever learn. Don't be afraid to experiment or try different approaches. Every mistake is simply another step toward growth.

- **Keep a Learning Journal:** Include your daily learnings, reflections, and thoughts. Gradually, your journal will turn into a proof of your development, and also an incentive to continue on the hard days.

- **Challenge:** Plan to learn one new thing each day for the next 30 days. It could be a new word, a fun fact, or a bit of a skill. This challenge would not only broaden your knowledge but also help to inculcate the habit of daily learning.

LEARNING FROM FAILURE AND ADAPT TO NEW CHALLENGES

Fear of failure is one of the most widespread fears, but the fact is that failure is one of the most effective teachers. Take a lesson from Thomas Edison, who became known for saying he had not failed, but found 10,000 ways not to make a light bulb.

Strategies to Learn from Failure

Reframe Failure: Instead of asking 'why did I fail?' ask 'what can I learn from this experience?' It turns every setback into a lesson because of this shift in perspective.

Keep Trying: Persistence is key. Know that everyone who is successful has many times failed before they achieved their goals. You are different because you are willing to keep trying.

Adapt and Adjust: Then if one thing doesn't work, change it and keep trying. You need to be flexible in your approach if you struggle to overcome the obstacles.

Challenge: Pick an embarrassing mistake you recently made and write down the lesson you learned from that. Think about how you will apply this lesson to future decisions. In time, this will start to feel natural and even necessary when it comes to failure.

PREPARING FOR THE FUTURE: CAREER, LIFE, AND BEYOND

It's not just about gaining knowledge—it's about preparing yourself for a successful future. As you grow, it's important to set goals that go beyond the classroom and reach into your personal and professional life.

How to Prepare for a Successful Future

- **Develop a Growth Plan:** Set clear learning goals for the next 1, 5, and 10 years. Include both short-term and long-term objectives to build a roadmap that keeps you focused and moving forward on your journey of continuous improvement.

- **Find Mentors:** Listen to the experienced ones that have already done what you want to achieve. They can give you invaluable advice, feedback and encouragement as you go about your journey.

- **Stay Flexible:** Learn new skills, simultaneously and immediately even if it isn't instantly useful. Today's skills can be the basis for tomorrow's success in our quickly changing world.

- **Invest in Yourself:** Make it a habit to grow your knowledge and skills. Take courses, read books, attend workshops, and explore online learning platforms. The more you pour into your own development, the more opportunities will come your way.

- **Challenge:** Choose three skills you want to learn in the next year. For each one, write down how you plan to learn it and what steps you'll take to start building it. This exercise will help you clarify your goals and kickstart your journey toward personal and professional growth.

Keep Growing and Keep Learning

Lifelong learning isn't just a phase—it's a mindset. When Emily realized that learning doesn't end at the school gate, she began to see just how much more there was to discover and achieve. Success isn't about knowing everything all at once; it's about how you approach learning—your willingness to grow, adapt, and keep moving forward.

Key Takeaways

- **Never Stop Learning:** The world is constantly changing—and so should you. Be open to shifting your perspective and remember: learning is a lifelong journey, not a final destination.

- **Stay Curious:** Ask questions, explore new ideas, and welcome different viewpoints. Curiosity is the spark that fuels growth.

- **Learn from Failure:** Every mistake holds a lesson. Instead of fearing failure, see it as a stepping stone that moves you closer to success.

- **Prepare for the Future:** Set meaningful goals, connect with mentors, stay flexible in how you learn, and most importantly—keep investing in yourself and your growth.

Being open to learning and embracing change is what turns learning into a lifelong superpower. In a world that's always evolving, it's the key to staying ahead. As you continue to grow, you'll gain new skills, build confidence, and with each lesson, move closer to becoming the best version of yourself.

Now that you've unlocked the secrets of lifelong learning and continuous improvement, it's time to bring it all together. The next step? Turning everything you've learned in this book into a practical action plan—a roadmap for lasting success. This isn't just a summary; it's a guide that helps you weave every strategy, from time management to growth mindset, into your daily routine.

Imagine having a step-by-step plan that not only reminds you of each skill but shows you exactly how to use it. Each chapter gave you tools to overcome challenges, stay focused, and keep growing—and now it's time to combine them into one powerful system.

Are you ready to see how everything fits together into a full-on strategy for progress? As we wrap up this chapter, take that next step with confidence—because your journey doesn't end here. It's just getting started.

YOUR JOURNEY STARTS NOW

You've made it to the end of this book—but really, this is just the beginning. This journey has been about helping you understand and strengthen your executive functioning skills—those behind-the-scenes powers that help you stay focused, organized, and in control of your life.

What you've learned here isn't just about tips and tricks. It's about building a mindset that will help you take control of your time, your focus, and your future. By now, you've built a toolkit of strategies to beat procrastination, manage your time, stay motivated, and handle everyday challenges with more confidence.

But here's the truth: knowledge doesn't mean much unless you *use* it.

One of the most important lessons you can carry with you is the power of self-awareness. Knowing how your brain works—what helps you focus, what distracts you, and what throws off your routine—is a game-changer. When you're honest with yourself about your strengths and struggles, you give yourself the ability to adapt and grow. Think of your brain like a muscle. The more you use it—especially with these tools—the stronger it gets. So whether it's turning off notifications, planning your day the night before, or just showing up and trying again after a setback, *every small step counts*.

Life won't always go according to plan, and that's okay. Flexibility is a skill, and like any skill, it can be developed. Being flexible means adjusting when things change and finding a new path instead of giving up. When something unexpected happens—like a change in schedule or a plan that falls apart—take a breath, reassess, and figure out your next best move. You've got what it takes to handle twists and turns.

Resilience is also key. There will be times when you forget your planner, fall behind on an assignment, or just feel unmotivated. What matters is how you bounce back. Instead of beating yourself up, use setbacks as learning experiences. What went wrong? What can you do differently next time? Every stumble is a step toward being more capable and prepared.

Your ability to focus, stay organized, and manage your time gets stronger the more you practice. Use checklists. Break big tasks into smaller ones. Set reminders. Review your goals often. These habits may feel small, but they have a big impact. Just like working out builds muscle, consistent effort builds the habits that make school (and life) easier to manage.

Accountability can help you stay on track. Whether it's a teacher, parent, coach, or friend, having someone who checks in and encourages you can make a big difference. Don't be afraid to reach out for support or share your goals. You're not in this alone—and you shouldn't have to figure everything out by yourself.

Your executive functioning journey is personal. Set goals that make sense for you, whether that's getting better at managing your time, staying focused in class, or remembering your assignments without feeling overwhelmed. Celebrate your progress, no matter how small. Success doesn't happen overnight—but every smart decision you make gets you closer to it.

Keep investing in yourself. Read books, watch videos, try productivity apps, or learn from people who've been where you are. The more you know, the more you grow. You've already proven you can stick with something important by making it to the end of this book. That says a lot about your dedication and potential.

Now, the real journey begins. Step out of your comfort zone, use the skills you've gained, and take control of your time, your goals, and your life. You *can* stay focused. You *can* get organized. You *can* handle challenges. And with consistent practice, you'll keep getting better.

You're not alone if staying on track feels tough sometimes— lots of teens struggle with it. But you've got what it takes to figure it out, step by step. Keep showing up for yourself. Keep learning. Keep growing.

So, what's your next step? Maybe it's reviewing a chapter that challenged you. Maybe it's setting one new goal. Or maybe it's just deciding to try again tomorrow.

Whatever it is, know this:

You've got what it takes.
You're capable of more than you think.
And your journey to success starts *right now.*

Here's to your continued progress, success, and the confident, capable future you're building—one smart decision at a time.

UNLOCKING EXECUTIVE FUNCTIONING SKILLS FOR TEENS

Now that you have the tools to master executive functioning, it's time to put everything into practice and share what you've learned with others.

Hey there, amazing reader!

Congratulations on finishing *Unlocking Executive Functioning Skills for Teens* by Kimberly Myrick! You've gained the skills to stay organized, manage your time, stay focused, and overcome obstacles. You're ready to take control of your future with confidence. But before you go, there's one more thing you can do to help others on their journey.

By leaving a review, you'll guide other teens who are looking to improve their executive functioning skills. Your honest feedback could be exactly what someone else needs to get started on their path to success.

Thank you for being part of this journey. The more we share what we've learned, the stronger we all become. Your review keeps this knowledge flowing and helps others unlock their potential.

Your biggest fan,

Kimberly Myrick

RESOURCES

Thank you for reading **Executive Functioning Skills for Teens**! To continue your journey toward better organization, focus, and time management, here are some helpful resources:

Books & Guides

- *The 7 Habits of Highly Effective Teens* by Sean Covey

- *Smart but Scattered Teens* by Peg Dawson & Richard Guare

- Barkley, R. A. (2020). *Executive functions: What they are, how they work, and why they evolved.* New York, NY: Guilford Press.

- Dweck, C. S. (2016). *Mindset: The new psychology of success.* New York, NY: Random House.

- Covey, S. R. (2020). *The 7 habits of highly effective teens.* New York, NY: Simon & Schuster.'

- *Atomic Habits* by James Clear (for building better habits)

- Myrick, K. (2025). *Unlocking social skills for teens: Practical strategies to build confidence and connect with others.*

- Teen Mentorship Program. (2023). Building resilience through peer support networks. Retrieved from https://www.teenmentorship.org

Apps & Tools for Productivity

- **Trello / Notion / Evernote** – For organizing tasks and projects

- **Google Calendar / Todoist** – For time management and scheduling

- **Pomodoro Timer Apps** – To improve focus using the Pomodoro Technique

- **Forest App / Freedom App** – To reduce digital distractions

Websites & Online Resources

- ADDitude Magazine – Expert advice on executive functioning and ADHD

- Khan Academy. (2023). *Study tips and time management strategies for students.* Retrieved from https://www.khanacademy.org

- MindTools – Tips on productivity, time management, and goal setting

- Khan Academy – Free educational resources to support learning

REFERENCES

Myrick, K. (2025). *Unlocking executive functioning skills for teens: Simple tools to improve focus, beat procrastination, and thrive in high school.*

American Psychological Association. (2023). *Executive functioning and adolescent development.* Retrieved from https://www.apa.org

Harvard Center for Education. (2023). *Adolescent brain development and executive functioning.* Retrieved from https://www.gse.harvard.edu

National Institute of Mental Health. (2023). *Understanding attention and focus in teens.* Retrieved from https://www.nimh.nih.gov

Smith, J. A., & Lee, R. T. (2022). Developing executive functioning skills in high school students. *Journal of Educational Psychology, 114* (3), 245–260. https://doi.org/10.1037/edu0000123

Wilson, L. (2021). *The teen's guide to time management: Strategies for success in high school and beyond.* New York, NY: Academic Press.

How a Growth Mindset Benefits Kids' Social-*Emotional* ... *https://* www.familius.com/growth-mindset-for-kids

American Psychological Association. (2020). *Publication manual of the American Psychological Association* (7th ed.).

Covey, S. (2014). *The 7 habits of highly effective teens.* Simon & Schuster.

Dawson, P., & Guare, R. (2018). *Smart but scattered teens: The "executive skills" program for helping teens reach their potential.* Guilford Press.

Clear, J. (2018). *Atomic habits: An easy & proven way to build good habits & break bad ones.* Avery.

Khan Academy. (n.d.). *Executive functioning and study skills.* Retrieved from https://www.khanacademy.org/

MindTools. (n.d.). *Time management & productivity strategies.* Retrieved from https://www.mindtools.com/

National Institute of Mental Health. (2021). *Understanding executive function.* Retrieved from https://www.nimh.nih.gov

Thank You for Reading!

If *Unlocking Executive Functioning Skills for Teens* helped you or someone you love, I'd be incredibly grateful if you left a quick review. Your feedback helps others find the book and supports more helpful resources for teens.

Leave a review on Amazon – it only takes a minute and makes a big difference!

Click Here to Review

Stay Connected

Want helpful tips, free teen guides, and bonus resources sent straight to your inbox?

Sign up for the newsletter and get access to:

★ A printable companion workbook
★ Exclusive updates and sneak peeks
★ Special offers and bonus content

kimberlymyrickauthor.com

Also by Kimberly Myrick

Unlocking Social Skills for Teens

Stay tuned for more empowering books designed to help teens grow, thrive, and succeed in every area of life!

Coming Soon
Unlocking Emotional Intelligence for Teens
Discover how to recognize emotions, build healthy relationships, and handle tough moments with confidence and calm.
Fall 2025